Karla S. Rugh

English Setters

Everything About Purchase, Care, Nutrition, and Behavior

Filled with Full-color Photographs

Illustrations by Tracy S. Fleckinger and Michele Earle-Bridges

BARRON'S

2 CONTENTS

MEET THE ENGLISH SETTER

The English Setter Family Tree

English Setters were used as trained bird dogs more than 400 years ago. These dogs were probably developed from crosses of Spanish Pointers, large Water Spaniels, and Springer Spaniels. The result was a handsome dog highly skilled at finding and pointing game in open country.

The early English Setters, or setter-spaniels, varied somewhat in their appearance. Some had short spaniel-type heads; others had heads that were longer with a more classic profile. They had curly coats, instead of the flat, feathered coat of today's setters.

Three distinct types of English Setters—the Laverack, Llewellin, and Ryman—have been developed. Although each type has specific talents and characteristics, all are good-looking dogs and talented hunters. In reality, few English Setters are exclusively one strain or the other.

All in the Family: Laverack and Llewellin Setters

Edward Laverack is credited with the development of the English Setter typified by the AKC breed standard. In 1825 he obtained two dogs, named Pronto and Old Moll, and used inbreed-

The English Setter (left), Gordon Setter (center), and Irish Setter are the three setter breeds recognized by the AKC.

ing to produce several outstanding English Setters. Laverack apparently bred his setters strictly for hunting. The appearance that brought the English Setter show ring success was secondary to hunting ability.

R. L. Purcell Llewellin of South Wales, developed another strain of English Setter. In the mid-1860s Llewellin obtained his first setters from Laverack. Llewellin tried for several years to develop a strain of English Setters that would be superior for field work. Finally, in 1871 he purchased Dan and Dick, sons of Duke and Rhoebe, who were descended from stock that was noted for outstanding field work. Llewellin bred Dan and Dick to his Laverack females and achieved his goal. The offspring quickly became popular with sportsmen in both England and North America.

Gladstone, one of the most important Llewellins of all time, was a son of Dan. His achievements as a top field performer and sire greatly contributed to the popularity of Llewellins. Count Noble was another prominent early Llewellin. The crossing of Count Noble to Gladstone's daughters established Llewellins as the dominant dogs in trial competitions.

The Llewellin English Setter is an intelligent dog with outstanding hunting abilities and a good disposition. Contrary to popular belief, Llewellins are marked and colored like any other English Setter. Llewellin Setters weigh about 50 pounds (23 kg), with a height of about 24 inches (61 cm). *The Field Dog Stud Book* recognizes Llewellins as those English Setters whose lineage traces back to the original Duke-Rhoebe-Laverack cross.

The Latest Development: Ryman Setters

Laverack and Llewellin setters were first imported to the United States in the late 1800s. In 1910 George Ryman set out to develop a line of English Setters that combined the Llewellin's field abilities with the Laverack's conformation. He began his breeding program with dogs from the Sir Roger DeCoverly-Sir Roger DeCoverly II bloodline, which had produced setters that were skilled hunters as well as bench competitors. Ryman achieved his goal, and his dogs became popular with sportsmen who wanted a setter to hunt as well as show. Ryman continued to build on the DeCoverly bloodlines, using prominent American bloodlines as well. He also incorporated bloodlines from imported bench and field champions. Many breeders have used Ryman dogs as foundation stock for the development of other lines.

Ryman Setters are good hunters, but not field trial experts like the Llewellins. Most Rymans are either orange or blue belton, although tricolors are fairly common. Males stand about 25 inches (63 cm) at the shoulder and weigh 60 to 65 pounds (27–29 kg). Females stand about 24 inches (61 cm) at the shoulder and are about 10 pounds (4.5 kg) lighter.

English Setter Registries

English Setters can be registered through one or more associations. The best known of these is probably the American Kennel Club (AKC). English Setters are also one of the recognized breeds of the United Kennel Club. Field-type English Setters, and other AKC-registrable sporting breeds except Irish Setters, can be registered in *The Field Dog Stud Book* (FDSB) (see Information, page 93). A U.S.-born dog that is registered with the FDSB and has an FDSB-registered sire and dam may be registered with the AKC, provided a three-generation FDSB certified pedigree accompanies the registration application. If the sire and dam of an FDSB-registered dog are registered with the AKC, standard application procedures must be followed to obtain AKC registration.

The English Setter Breed Standard

The AKC's Official Standard for the English Setter describes the temperament and physical characteristics of the ideal English Setter. The breed is judged according to this standard in AKC-recognized dog shows. Don't be discouraged if your English Setter doesn't measure up to every aspect of the standard—few dogs do. That won't keep your setter from being your own personal pick for Best of Show every time!

I've interpreted the standard for this book. The official standard can be found in *The Complete Dog Book,* available in many libraries. Updated breed standards are also periodically published in *Dog World* magazine (for the address, see Information, page 93).

General Appearance

The English Setter is an elegant, substantial, and well-balanced dog that combines strength, stamina, grace, and style. The coat should be flat and well-feathered. The English Setter should move freely and smoothly, with a good front leg reach and a powerful drive from the rear quarters. Males should be masculine without being coarse; females should be feminine without being overly refined. The overall "picture" is more important than any single feature. Any extreme feature that distorts the breed type must be faulted.

Head

The English Setter's head should be in proportion to the body. It should be long and lean with a well-defined stop (the "step up" from the muzzle to the skull). The top of muzzle, top of skull, and bottom of lower jaw should be parallel when viewed from the side.

Skull: The skull should be oval when viewed from above. Of medium width, it should have no coarseness, and should be slightly wider where the ears join the head than at the brow. The length of skull from the stop to the occiput (the upper part of the skull just before it joins the neck) should equal the muzzle length. The occipital protuberance (a raised occiput that is characteristic of some of the sporting and hound breeds) should be moderately defined.

Muzzle: The English Setter's muzzle should be long and square when viewed from the side. It should have good depth with square, fairly drooping flews (upper lips). The muzzle should be level from the eyes to the tip of the nose. The muzzle width should be proportional with the width of the skull and shouldn't vary from nose to stop.

Nose: The nose should be fully pigmented dark brown or black, with large, wide-set nostrils.

Foreface: The English Setter's foreface (the front part of the skull that joins the cranium)

should be well-chiseled under the eyes, with smooth, trim cheeks.

Teeth: A scissors bite (the inner surfaces of the upper front teeth touch the outer surfaces of the lower front teeth when the mouth is closed) is ideal, but an even bite (the upper and lower front teeth meet with no overlap) is also acceptable.

Eyes: The eyes should be dark brown, bright, almost round, and somewhat large. Neither deepset or protruding, they should give the face a mild, intelligent expression. The eyelid rims should be dark and completely pigmented, fitting closely so that the haw (the third eyelid or nictitating membrane at the eye's inner corner) does not show.

Ears: The English Setter's ears should be set well back, at or below eye level. The ears should be moderately long, with slightly rounded ends and moderately thin leathers. When the dog is relaxed, the ears should lie close to the head.

Neck, Topline, Body

Neck: The English Setter's neck should be long, graceful, muscular, and lean. It should arch at the crest and join the head cleanly at the base of the skull. The base should blend smoothly into the shoulders. There should be no excess loose skin under the throat.

Topline: During gaiting or standing, the topline should be level or sloped slightly downward, forming a graceful outline.

Forechest: The forechest should be well-developed, with the breastbone projecting slightly.

Chest: The English Setter's chest should be deep, but should not interfere with foreleg action.

Above: English Setters have been used as bird dogs for more than 400 years.
Left: English Setters are energetic, but sometimes they like to lie down and watch the world go by.

Ribs: The ribs should spring gradually toward the middle of the body, then taper toward the end of the chest cavity.

Back: The English Setter's back should be straight and strong where it connects with the loin.

Loin: The loin should be strong, moderately long and slightly arched. The "waist" should be moderately defined.

Hips: The croup (the top of the hips just in front of the tail) should be nearly flat. The hip bones should be set wide apart, forming rounded hips that blend smoothly into the hind legs.

Tail: The English Setter's tail should be carried straight and level with the back. It should be sufficiently long enough to just reach the hock (or slightly less). The tail should be feathered with straight, silky hair.

These Laverack English Setters are orange belton (left) and blue belton, two of the AKC-recognized colors of English Setters.

Llewellin English Setters have been bred to be excellent hunters.

English Setters are naturally graceful and athletic.

The external anatomy of the English Setter.

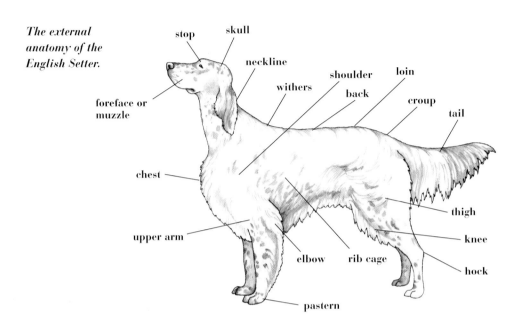

stop
skull
neckline
shoulder
loin
withers
back
croup
tail
foreface or muzzle
chest
thigh
upper arm
knee
elbow
rib cage
hock
pastern

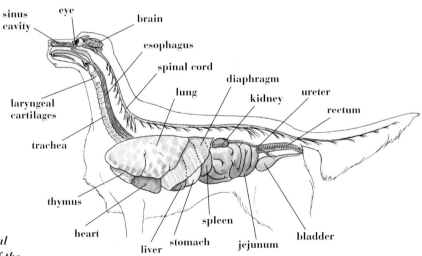

sinus cavity
eye
brain
esophagus
spinal cord
diaphragm
lung
kidney
ureter
rectum
laryngeal cartilages
trachea
thymus
heart
liver
stomach
spleen
jejunum
bladder

The internal anatomy of the English Setter.

Forequarters

Shoulders: The shoulder blades, well laid back, should blend smoothly with the body. The upper arm and shoulder blade should be equal in length and form a nearly right angle. The shoulders should be fairly close together at the tips of the shoulder blades.

Forelegs: The forelegs should be straight and parallel from either the front or side. The elbows should remain parallel when the dog is standing or moving. The arms should be flat, with well-developed muscles. The foreleg bones should be sturdy but not coarse.

Pasterns and Feet: The English Setter should have short, strong, nearly round pasterns that slope very slightly forward from perpendicular. The feet should face forward, with strong well-arched toes close together. The footpads should be well-developed and tough. Dewclaws may be removed.

Hindquarters

The English Setter should have wide muscular thighs and well-developed lower thighs. The pelvis and upper thigh should be equal in length and form a nearly right angle. The stifle and hock joints should be well-bent and strong. The lower thigh should be only slightly longer than the upper thigh. The rear pastern should be short, strong, nearly round and perpendicular to the ground. When seen from the rear, the hind legs should be straight and parallel to each other. The hock joints should remain parallel when the dog is standing or moving.

Coat

The English Setter's coat should be flat with no curliness or wooliness. The feathering on the ears, chest, abdomen, thighs, legs, and tail should be long but shouldn't hide conformation and movement or affect the appearance or function as a sporting dog.

Markings: The English Setter's coat consists of a white ground color intermingled with darker hairs. The resultant "belton" markings vary from distinct flecking to roan shading; all-over flecking is preferred. Colored patches on the head and ears are acceptable; heavy patches on the body are undesirable.

Colors

The accepted colors for English Setters include orange belton (white with light reddish markings), blue belton (white with black markings), tricolor (blue belton with tan on the face and legs), lemon belton (white with golden markings), and liver belton (white with dark brown markings).

Movement and Carriage

The English Setter should move effortlessly and gracefully, with a long forward reach and strong rear drive. The tail should be lively and the head carried proudly, although it may be carried slightly lower when moving to allow for greater reach of forelegs. The back should be strong and firm, without any rolling motion.

Size

Males should be about 25 inches tall at the shoulder. Females should be about 24 inches tall.

Temperament

The English Setter should be gentle, affectionate, and friendly, without shyness, fear, or viciousness.

UNDERSTANDING YOUR ENGLISH SETTER

It's hard to believe that the aristocratic English Setter lying peacefully at your feet is the not-so-distant cousin of the wolf, but it's true. All domesticated dogs descended from wolves, and our pet dogs have retained more wild instincts than you might realize.

Laws of the Pack

Wolves are social animals that live together in extended family groups called packs. Each pack inhabits a specific territory, the boundaries of which the male wolves mark by urination. The territory is fiercely guarded against wolves from other packs. Pack members frequently work together to benefit the entire pack, such as when hunting and raising their young.

The pack's social order is a hierarchy with one dominant, or alpha, male and other subordinate males. Subordinate males may be dominant over more subordinate males. The females have a similar social structure. Each wolf's behavior is dictated by its rank in the pack. For example, the alpha male eats first, chooses his mate first (usually the alpha female), and is treated with respect by all the subordinate wolves—at least until another male challenges his authority. This "pecking order" continues all the way down to the most subordinate wolf in the pack.

Both juvenile and adult English Setters show strong hunting instincts.

Changes in the pack hierarchy occur relatively frequently. Each wolf tries to become dominant over as many other wolves as possible, with the ultimate goal of becoming the alpha male or female. A wolf's position in the pack depends on how effectively it fends off the challenges from the wolves that are subordinate to it.

Canine Body Language

Dogs and their relatives communicate by complex and sometimes subtle body movements that are readily understood by other dogs. Dogs also use body language when interacting with humans and other animals. Understanding canine body language will help you understand what your English Setter is trying to tell you.

Almost everyone is familiar with the way a happy dog acts.

✔ A happy dog acknowledges the dominance of the individual (dog or human) it is approaching by crouching slightly. The ears will be back, the gaze soft and indirect, which is an expression of subordinance. The tail, which is usually wagging, is carried low.

✔ If the dog is approaching an individual that is much more dominant, it may roll over on its back to expose its abdomen. This is the most submissive posture that a dog can adopt. Even a very aggressive dog generally will not attack a dog displaying this behavior.

✔ An aggressive, dominant dog approaches another individual tensely, with an upright posture. With its head up, it issues a visual challenge by making direct eye contact. The tail is held stiffly erect with little wagging. The lips may be drawn back in a partial snarl. If the dominant dog is approaching another dog, the two may stand motionless at right angles to one another in a type of canine showdown. At this point, canine etiquette dictates that one dog must back down and demonstrate appropriate subordinate behavior. If this does not occur, the dogs will fight until one has established dominance.

Nervous Dogs

Nervous dogs may appear either submissive or aggressive depending on the situation. Most often, a nervous dog exhibits submissive behavior, unless it perceives that its submissive signals are not being respected. Even then, the nervous dog usually first tries to run away. If it can't escape, the submissive dog may then threaten to snap or bite, but never with the body language of a truly dominant aggressive dog. Nervous dogs that become aggressive

under such circumstances are often referred to as *fear biters*.

Your English Setter may not exhibit any of these behaviors to the extent they have been described, but if you watch closely you'll see canine body language every day. How your setter acts may also depend on the situation and who's involved. For instance, your English Setter may exhibit mainly happy, submissive mannerisms toward you, yet become dominant and aggressive around other dogs.

Today's Pack

The human family is the domesticated dog's pack. Just as in the wolf pack, there is one dominant member—usually an adult—and one or more subordinate members. The pack's territory is the home and surrounding property, although some dogs may claim as pack territory certain highly frequented areas, such as the neighborhood park.

Your English Setter's position in the family pack is one of subordination to all humans, regardless of age or gender. To a dog, this is reassuring, because in a pack all members know their place. If the social order is understood, your English Setter will know how to act. Dogs are confused by inconsistency, for example, when dominant behavior is allowed on one day, yet punished on the next.

The aggressive dog has a direct gaze, stiff gait, and erect tail. The lips may be drawn back in a partial snarl. A dog exhibiting this behavior could be extremely dangerous to dogs and humans.

*A subordinate dog usually adopts
a crouching position when
approaching a more dominant dog.*

"Top Dog"

It's easy to establish dominance with some dogs—these cheerful followers just naturally accept their position. Other dogs, more independent, stubborn, or ambitious, will constantly challenge your authority. So how do you prove that you're "top dog"?

Think like a wolf. Remember that the alpha pack member makes all the decisions and gets first pick of food, affection, *everything.*

1. For starters, don't be overly affectionate. In a canine pack, the dominant member displays little affection for subordinates; instead, the subordinate members approach the dominant member and display affection. So don't just walk over to your English Setter and start petting him. Call him to you and pet him only after he has obeyed a simple command, such as *"Sit."*

2. Don't automatically respond to your setter's every wish, such as demands to go for a walk. As the dominant pack member, *you* decide those things.

3. Don't feed him before you eat—in a pack, the dominant members eat first.

4. Don't let your English Setter put his paws in your lap when you sit down. To a dog this is a show of dominance, similar to the behavior displayed when a dominant dog puts its front paws on top of the subordinate dog's back.

5. Don't allow your setter to be physically higher than you, such as might occur if he sits on your lap (it's not that unusual even with

setter-sized dogs!) or the two of you have a "friendly" wrestling match on the floor. Physical elevation is a strongly dominant canine behavior. If you permit it, you're sure to confuse your setter about his place in the family pack.

By now you're probably thinking that all of this dominant-subordinate stuff doesn't sound like any fun at all. Here's the good news: You probably won't have to use all of the above tactics to establish and maintain your dominance with your English Setter. Dogs are very good at interpreting social signals. Just acting like you're in charge goes a long way toward convincing them that you're the boss. If, however, your setter starts challenging your authority, it's nice to know how to regain it.

Your English Setter and Other Family Members

Your English Setter's relationship with each family member will depend on whether your setter feels he is dominant or subordinate to that person. For instance, a dog may accept the man as the dominant pack member, yet view the woman and especially children as subordinate. When this happens, the man is readily obeyed, but the other family members

Above: In any group of dogs, there's a structured social order with dominant and subordinate members.
Left: Whatever the breed has become today, English Setters were first and foremost hunters.

encounter varying degrees of resistance to their requests. Sometimes the man and woman are acknowledged as dominant, but the children are treated as subordinate by the dog. None of these situations is acceptable; in a human/dog "pack," the dog is subordinate to *every* human family member—even children. If the dog displays dominant behavior toward certain human family members, those persons should receive extra attention from the person the dog perceives as dominant (in a wolf pack,

Above: Your English Setter should quietly tolerate grooming and examination. This hunter is checking his English Setter's footpads for burrs.
Left: Make sure your English Setter has a variety of safe toys to play with.
Below: Dogs and cats don't have to be enemies. Many of them get along quite well, especially if they've been raised together.

association of a dominant wolf with a subordinate one elevates the status of the subordinate wolf). The dominant family member should also ignore the dog as much as possible, reinforcing the dog's subordinate social position.

Some dogs exhibit neither consistently dominant nor subordinate behavior with children. This often happens when the dog can't interpret the child's actions or when the child doesn't understand, or simply ignores the behavioral language of the dog. Sometimes it's due to activity level; the boisterous activity of high-energy children may intimidate shy dogs. Even a normally quiet, friendly dog should be constantly supervised while around young children—for the dog's protection as well as the child's. Dogs prone to displaying dominant behavior often cannot ever be completely trusted around children of any age.

Your English Setter and Other Pets

The meeting of two dogs that are strangers is accompanied by all sorts of complex social signals. Whether your English Setter views another dog as a friend or foe depends on several factors, including the age and gender of the dog, where the meeting occurs, and whether either owner is present. In general, dogs of different maturity stages, such as puppies meeting adults, establish a friendly relationship quicker than dogs of similar maturity, unless both are puppies. Dogs of different genders also seem to accept one another more readily, although this varies. For instance, a female with puppies may be intolerant of a male dog. Two dogs often get along better if the meeting takes place away from either dog's

territory. Problems can arise, however, if either, or both, of the dogs decides that a frequently visited public location, such as a park, is part of its territory. Some dogs get along better when their owners are not around, presumably because there are fewer jealousy problems.

How your English Setter behaves with other pets will depend your setter's personality, the other pet and its personality, and the particular situation. Keeping free-ranging domestic birds, such as ducks and chickens, if you have an English Setter is not recommended—those bird dog instincts may just be too hard to resist! Many dogs get along quite well with cats, especially if they were raised together. Sometimes a pet, such as a rabbit, is treated gently if it's inactive, yet pursued vigorously if it runs.

You should constantly supervise your English Setter with other pets, at least at first, especially if there is a great size difference or one of the animals is capable of inflicting serious damage on the other.

Why Did My English Setter Do That?

"When I take my English Setter for a walk, why does he try to urinate on every tree and shrub on the block?" Male dogs (and even some females) don't just urinate to relieve themselves; they're marking the boundaries of their territory, real or otherwise. If another dog has urinated in that same place, marking his territory, your dog will try to do the same to let other dogs know this is *his* turf. You don't have to put up with this behavior. Move your setter along with a reprimand and a quick tug on the leash.

"Why did my English Setter snap at me when I brushed her ears?" It's easy to attribute

this sort of behavior to sensitive skin or some other delicate condition, but your dog may simply be trying to advance her social position to one of dominance over you. Use some or all of the methods outlined above to remind her that she is still subordinate. In addition, teach her to obey a simple command, such as *"Sit."* After she has learned the command, make her sit while you gently brush a part of her body where it least bothers her. If she tolerates the brushing, praise her. If she objects, stop brushing and repeat the command to sit (re-establishing your dominance), then continue brushing. Gradually increase the duration and extent of brushing, until she'll let you brush any part of her body.

"Why did my English Setter growl at my four-year-old when she picked up one of his dog toys that he wasn't even playing with?" Your English Setter's behavior indicates that he regards your daughter as subordinate to him—the wrong attitude in a human household, where the dog is subordinate to *all* humans, even young children. Because your daughter cannot assert her dominance over your dog, you should reprimand your setter. This will elevate your daughter's status in the eyes of your dog. You should also reinforce the family pack "pecking order" by using some of the previously described techniques for establishing dominance. Young children should never be left alone with a dog that displays any dominant behavior toward them.

"Why does my adult English Setter always pick on our four-month-old English Setter puppy?" Your older English Setter is asserting his or her dominance over the younger one. Although both dogs should be subordinate to all the humans in your family, your setters will never be social equals—one will always be more dominant. Because canine social status is not constant, the dominant dog must re-establish dominance whenever the subordinate dog tries to gain it. It's normal for the subordinate dog to frequently challenge the authority of the dominant one. As much as possible, let your dogs establish their own social order between themselves. Don't try to defend the subordinate dog unless there's danger of serious injury (a rare occurrence), because this will disrupt the social order between the dogs and ultimately cause more conflict.

"Why does my English Setter growl at my husband when he hugs me or even just sits next to me?" Your English Setter's behavior indicates that he thinks he has a pair relationship with you. Dogs with this attitude usually treat the wife with particular deference and view the husband as a rival, a situation that can be very frightening if the dog becomes aggressive toward the husband. This inappropriate behavior can often be thwarted without violence if you "reject" your setter by pointedly and persistently ignoring him. In addition, all dog-care duties should be turned over to your husband until the correct social order is re-established. If you and your husband feel that you cannot regain control using these methods, don't hesitate to seek the advice of a canine behavior specialist.

So you want to get a dog. Perhaps you remember the dog that was your best buddy when you were young. Perhaps you have a friend who has a dog and you envy their special relationship. Perhaps you've recently retired and want a dog to help fill up those extra hours. Perhaps you just like dogs.

All of these reasons are important, but none of them is sufficient enough to get a dog without considering the responsibilities. Are you committed to providing food, shelter, grooming, veterinary care, love, and companionship for the next 10 to 12 years or more? If you're not, don't get a dog. If, on the other hand, you're willing to give it your best effort, get ready for a wonderful adventure!

Before you start looking for an English Setter, take some time to decide what characteristics your ideal dog should have. That way, when you start dog-shopping, you'll be less likely to go home with a dog that really wasn't what you wanted.

What Type of Setter?

The diversity of English Setters lets you select a setter that has just the characteristics you most desire. Regardless of their other talents, they all make good pets.

Selecting an English Setter can be difficult. How could you choose between these two?

The Laverack Setter is the classic setter most often seen in dog shows. Tall and elegant, it typifies the AKC breed standard. A Laverack Setter would be a good choice if you plan to show your English Setter in AKC dog shows in bench (conformation) classes. Laverack Setters are capable hunters, but they are not as talented in the field as the Llewellin or Ryman Setters.

Llewellin Setters are shorter than the other two strains. These handsome dogs are fast and athletic, the hunting experts of the English Setter breed. If you want a talented hunting dog or one you can show in field trials or hunting tests, a Llewellin would be a good choice.

The Ryman Setter possesses some of the characteristics of the other two strains. For instance, the overall conformation and refinement of the Ryman Setter is similar to that of the Laverack, though Rymans are somewhat smaller. The Ryman's hunting talents are generally better than those of the Laverack, but do not equal those of the Llewellins. The Ryman Setter is a good choice for someone who wants a good-looking dog that is also a talented hunter.

Pet Quality, Show Quality, or Breeding Quality?

Being a pet is the most important job your English Setter will have. If you don't plan to show your English Setter, you can save some money by purchasing a pet-quality setter instead of a show-quality one. Many English Setters that aren't suitable for showing make terrific pets. They don't have anything wrong with them, they just lack the near-perfect physical characteristics required for show-ring success.

If you plan to show your dog, you should purchase the best English Setter you can possibly afford—but *never* compromise temperament for physical perfection. A show-quality setter usually has parents that have had successful show careers, although that doesn't necessarily guarantee a show-quality puppy. Unless you're an English Setter expert, you should rely on a knowledgeable breeder's opinion about the best puppy for showing. Keep in mind, however, that no one can pick a winner every time.

If you hope to one day breed your English Setter, you should look for a dog that is, or will become, an outstanding example of the breed. Many experts recommend that only a dog of the very best show quality be used for breeding, because that dog's characteristics will be passed on to many generations of English Setters. Breeding-quality dogs are usually quite expensive. They are usually selected as adults because their physical characteristics, as well as their show and/or breeding record, can be readily evaluated. An experienced English Setter breeder can help you select a breeding-quality dog.

Puppy or Adult?

Whether you decide to adopt an English Setter puppy or an adult will depend on your expectations, your physical capabilities, your anticipated time commitment, and even your family's preference.

Puppies are hard to resist; they're cute and cuddly, make those sweet puppy sounds when you hold them close, and bond quickly to their caregivers. On the other hand, puppies are also a lot of work. They eat several times a day. They chew things up—things you don't want chewed up, such as your brand-new shoes, and things that aren't good for them, such as your pincushion. They must be housebroken. They need supervision—both inside and outside.

Adopting an adult English Setter has its rewards.

✔ It's easier to evaluate an adult dog's personality. Adult dogs are usually calmer and more settled than puppies.

✔ Most adult dogs have outgrown the chewing stage.

✔ Adult dogs are usually housebroken.

✔ If you want a show- or breeding-quality setter, it's easier to assess the physical characteristics of an adult than a puppy.

✔ Some adult setters may have show-ring experience.

✔ An adult dog may be somewhat slower than a puppy to fully adopt its humans, especially if the dog was strongly attached to its former owners. Nevertheless, with a little extra time and attention, the adult English Setter will become thoroughly devoted to its new owner.

Male or Female?

Male dogs are usually somewhat more aggressive than females, but this depends on the individual's temperament and the situation (a female with puppies can be quite aggressive). All English Setters love to roam, but males usually roam more than females, marking their territory by urinating on trees and other upright objects. Some males may raise their leg in the house, although this shouldn't be a problem with a reliably housebroken dog.

Female English Setters, like females of other breeds, come into season ("heat" or estrus) about twice a year. During this time, they must be isolated from male dogs to avoid an unwanted litter. A female in heat has a bloody vaginal discharge that may stain carpets and furniture.

Puppy Sources

Depending on where you live, you may have several puppy sources available to you. You can contact an English Setter breeder, talk to the folks down the street whose English Setter just had a litter, or visit the pet shop.

English Setter Breeders

For selection and quality, your best source for a new puppy or dog is probably an English Setter breeder. Breeders are dedicated to improving the English Setter breed. Because their reputation depends on the dogs they breed and sell, breeders work hard to make sure that their puppies receive proper nutrition, socialization, and health care. In addition, professional breeders maintain complete records for each dog.

Breeders usually have several puppies and dogs from which to choose. Prices range from rather reasonable for a pet-quality puppy to very expensive for a breeding-quality adult dog. Responsible breeders try to match the right dog or puppy to the right owner. Most breeders are also good sources of advice and information.

You can often find local English Setter breeders by checking newspaper classified ads

CHECKLIST

Spaying/Neutering

Gender-related disadvantages can be remedied by spaying or neutering ("altering"), surgical sterilization procedures that are performed by a veterinarian. Show dogs are not spayed or neutered, because altered dogs cannot be shown in conformation (bench) shows. If you purchase a pet-quality English Setter, I strongly urge you to have it spayed or neutered.

✔ Spaying or neutering won't change your dog's personality or cause obesity, unless you provide too many treats and not enough exercise.

✔ Spaying and neutering also have significant health benefits, such as decreasing the incidence of mammary cancer in females and certain diseases of the prostate and testicles in males.

✔ Altered dogs usually stay closer to home, which decreases exposure to such dangers as cars, vicious dogs, and dogs with communicable diseases.

✔ Finally, by spaying or neutering your English Setter, you can help reduce the number of unwanted dogs in this country. Each day, thousands of healthy puppies and dogs are killed because there are no homes for them. Responsible dog owners control their dog's reproductive potential by spaying or neutering.

A Llewellin-type English Setter would be a good choice if you enjoy hunting. Below: Proven show dogs can be quite expensive, but you should purchase the best one you can afford, especially if you plan to breed it.

Above: If you adopt an adult English Setter, you'll have a great companion without having to go through the hassles of raising a puppy.
Right: For many people, selecting a dog really means selecting a puppy.

English Setters come in several different sizes and colors.

(there will be "backyard breeders" here, too), local dog clubs, or veterinarians. For a national search, you can consult one of the major dog magazines, such as *Dog World* or *Dog Fancy* (see Information, page 93). Searching nation-wide is impractical for many prospective dog owners; most don't want to purchase a dog or puppy sight unseen and ship it to its new home. However, if you're reasonably sure the breeder will have the perfect setter, you may not mind making the trip and bringing your new friend home yourself. A distant breeder may also know someone in your area who raises English Setters.

Backyard Breeders

Another potential puppy source is the "back-yard breeder," someone who breeds his or her English Setter just to raise a litter of puppies. Selecting one of these puppies has some advantages. They're often well socialized, since they've been raised in a home situation. The puppies usually haven't been around many other dogs and the germs and parasites they carry. On the other hand, the health care of the puppies may be variable, depending on whether the owner has gone to the effort and expense of having them vaccinated and dewormed. You'll probably find only pet-quality puppies in a backyard litter. If a pet-quality setter is just what you're looking for, however, your new best friend may be right down the street.

Retail Pet Shops

If you shop for an English Setter puppy at a retail pet shop, you should evaluate the same factors that you would if you were buying a puppy from a private source. Pet shops should be willing and able to answer questions about the puppy's origins, parentage, early care and socialization, and care and handling since it arrived at the pet shop. Health records, pedigree, and registration papers (or application) should also be available. Some shops allow you to return a puppy that doesn't pass a veterinarian's evaluation. Some also have attractive package deals, in which basic puppy care items are included with the purchase of a puppy.

Picking a Puppy

The ideal age to adopt a puppy is between eight and twelve weeks. Puppies this age are usually weaned, eating well, and energetic. They adapt quickly to their new homes and form strong attachments to their new family. Follow these steps:

1. When you arrive at the puppies' home, take a look around. Is it neat and clean? Is there a safe, fenced yard for the puppies? Do the dogs look healthy and well-cared for? If you can answer yes to all these questions, go ahead and look at the puppies; however, if the facilities are messy, unsafe, or dirty, and the dogs appear to be unhealthy or neglected, look elsewhere for your puppy.

2. Before you meet the puppies, ask the breeder about their health care. Have they had their first immunizations? Have they been wormed? Have any of them been sick or injured?

3. When the breeder shows you the puppies, observe them as a group before you evaluate them individually. Are they active and playful? Do any seem unusually quiet or shy? Are any noticeably smaller than the others?

4. Sit down on the floor or ground and call the puppies, using your friendliest voice.

Eliminate from consideration any puppy that doesn't come running to you. Check the other puppies over carefully. Are some friendlier than the others? These are the puppies you'll want to examine further. Don't consider any puppy that seems timid or nervous.

5. Now pick up each puppy and examine it. The puppy should have clear eyes that are free from discharge. Its nose shouldn't be runny. Its gums should be a healthy pink, never pale.

A rounded tummy is normal, but the puppy shouldn't be potbellied, which might indicate roundworm infestation.

Check for an umbilical hernia, a small soft swelling near its "belly button." Umbilical hernias, which usually don't cause any problems unless they're quite large, can be repaired surgically. This isn't a problem in dogs that will be altered, but some veterinarians won't repair an umbilical hernia on a dog that might be shown or bred, because it's an inheritable condition.

Male puppies should have both testicles in the scrotum by 12 weeks of age. This may be difficult to assess because at this age the testicles can be pulled up into the body when the puppy is nervous. A dog with an undescended testicle (cryptorchidism) can't be shown in AKC dog shows. It is considered unethical for a veterinarian to correct this condition by any means other than castration. For a dog that will be neutered anyway, an undescended testicle is not a major defect, although abdominal surgery will be needed to remove the undescended testicle. (The undescended testicle should always be removed because abdominally retained testicles have an increased incidence of cancer.)

The puppy's anal area should be clean and dry, with no sign of irritation, which could indicate diarrhea.

6. Notice how each baby setter reacts to you as you examine it. The puppy should not be timid, but should accept you as a dominant figure. It should tolerate your examination without protesting or nipping (expect some wiggling!). If a puppy protests vigorously or tries to bite, eliminate it from your search. You don't want a puppy that rolls over on its back at your every move, but you don't want one that's always challenging you either. The ideal puppy is one that's friendly, outgoing, and willing to accept you as its leader.

Once you've selected your puppy, you and the breeder will need to discuss price and any conditions of the sale. The breeder may give you the registration papers or forms immediately, especially if you've chosen a show- or breeding-quality puppy. He or she may retain the papers of a pet-quality puppy until you've had it neutered. The breeder will probably want periodic updates on how you and your English Setter are getting along, especially if you plan to show your dog.

RAISING YOUR ENGLISH SETTER

Now that you've adopted an English Setter, you and your canine companion are probably both feeling a little nervous about your new life together. For your setter, everything's new—new house, new yard, new family. You may be feeling a bit overwhelmed too. Your English Setter will depend on you for every-thing—food, shelter, health care, companion-ship—for the rest of his or her life. But it's not all work. There's a lot of fun involved, and a lot of love and companionship too.

Essential Equipment

Dish and bowl: Your English Setter will need a food dish and a water bowl. They don't need to be fancy or expensive, just practical. Wide-based dog bowls made of crockery, plastic, or stainless steel can be used for both food and water. Crockery bowls work well because they're heavy and can't be easily tipped over. Some stores carry suction-footed racks for food and water bowls.

Carrier or crate: You'll also need a carrier or crate for your puppy's indoor bed. Your best choice will probably be one that's made of molded plastic or wire mesh. Mesh carriers can be placed on wooden blocks or rails, which allows urine to drain out if your puppy should

Your English Setter will depend on you for food, shelter, health care, and companionship.

have an "accident." Mesh isn't as comfortable as a solid floor, but most dogs don't seem to mind as long as they have a soft blanket to curl up on. If you choose a plastic carrier, you may be able to purchase a mesh floor for it. The carrier or crate should be large enough so an adult English Setter can stand up and move around in it. Try to get one that will fit in your car; you'll need it when you travel with your setter.

Collar and leash: A simple buckle-on nylon collar, preferably an inexpensive one (it will be quickly outgrown), will be fine for your puppy. You can select a higher-quality nylon or leather leash, since this is a "one-size-fits-all" item.

Before You Bring Your Puppy Home

Before you bring your new English Setter puppy home, you'll need to puppy-proof your house, or at least the areas your puppy will have access to. This can be challenging; most puppies are naturally curious explorers. Still, if you combine puppy-proofing with supervision you should be able to keep your little investi-gator safe.

✔ Unplug all nonessential electrical cords; hide any essential ones behind furniture, if possible. A puppy can receive a nasty shock from a plugged-in electrical cord and, for some reason, canine youngsters seem irresistibly attracted to them.

✔ Puppies like to put everything in their mouths, so remove potential choking hazards—paper clips, marbles, and such—from your puppy's area. Don't leave things like string, yarn, or thread where your puppy can get to them. If chewed on and swallowed, these materials can cause severe digestive tract damage, which often requires surgery to correct.

✔ Some houseplants, such as philodendron and pothos, are toxic to dogs. Other plants can cause digestive tract upsets if your puppy munches on the leaves or flowers. Instead of worrying about which plants are toxic and which aren't, it's simpler to move them out of your puppy's area until he outgrows the urge to "browse."

✔ Keep products such as paint thinner, antifreeze, cleaning supplies, and pesticides—all potentially fatal—out of your puppy's area. You'd think that puppies would stay far away from these foul-smelling compounds, but they don't.

A Setter Spot

Your English Setter will need a special spot for a "den"—a place to eat and sleep. It doesn't need to be large (a laundry room, for instance) or even necessarily a room (a kitchen corner will do), but it should be in a quiet place away from major household activity. I recommend starting right out using a roomy carrier or crate, lined with newspapers and soft towels, as a bed. That way, if you use the direct method of housebreaking, your puppy will already be used to staying in a carrier (see HOW-TO: Housebreaking, page 38). Using a carrier as a bed will also compel your young setter to stay in bed at night—remember to latch the door—and teach him that he has his own place to sleep. Make sure the carrier has a water holder so your puppy always has free access to water. Once you've decided where your puppy's special spot will be, leave the carrier there unless some unforeseen circumstance (not a lonesome puppy) dictates a change in location. If possible, place the carrier in an area that is somewhat removed from your bedroom. That way, you can hear your puppy if he cries at night, but he won't be howling right outside your bedroom door.

Welcome Home

Your English Setter puppy is bound to be a little nervous when you first bring him home. First of all, show him his new bed and food and water dishes (filled). Then let him decide what he wants to do. A timid puppy may want to stay right by your side, while a bolder setter may immediately venture forth to investigate his new home. Don't let the family interfere during his exploration. They can watch, of course, but as much as possible let your puppy pick his own pace and activities. For the time being, move your other dogs and cats out of the puppy's area; introductions will be easier on another, less exciting day. And don't get upset if your new buddy has an "accident"—that's pretty normal for an excited puppy.

Setter Down

Your English Setter puppy probably won't sleep very well the first night. After all, he's in new surroundings and he's probably never slept by himself before. So do you give in and just this once take him to bed with you or maybe just this once bring his carrier-bed into your bedroom? No and no, because "just this once" can very quickly turn into "all the time." The quickest and easiest way to teach your puppy to sleep in his own bed in his own area is to have him do it from the very beginning. You're also teaching him that he can't always be with you. If he doesn't learn that lesson early, future separations could be very traumatic.

When it's time for bed, after a snack and a trip outside, take your English Setter baby to his carrier, fluff up his blanket and put him in the carrier. Then tell him goodnight, close the carrier door, and leave. Don't go back unless you hear an alarming noise, beyond puppy barking or whining, such as the carrier falling over. Your puppy will undoubtedly cry, and you'll feel like a heartless meanie when you stay away. But remember, if you respond to his cries, he'll learn that all he has to do is cry loud enough and you'll come to him. If you absolutely can't resist checking on him, wait until he stops fussing, however briefly, and then go to him, praising him for being quiet. Check him quickly and leave.

House Rules

Soon after you bring your new puppy home, you'll need to decide whether there will be areas that are off-limits to your English Setter. If you decide to restrict your puppy's access to some areas, you'll need to firmly and consistently enforce those limits. If there are no doors you can close, it may help to put up removable gates or barriers. If gates or barriers aren't convenient, you'll need to watch carefully for "trespassing." When your puppy enters a restricted area, pick him up, reprimand him

CHECKLIST

Poisonous Plants

Below is a brief listing of some of the more commonly encountered poisonous plants that are grown inside the house or in the yard. For a complete listing of poisonous indoor and outdoor plants and their level of toxicity, consult your veterinarian.

✔ Amaryllis
✔ Asparagus Fern
✔ Azalea
✔ Bird of Paradise
✔ Boston Ivy
✔ Caladium
✔ Chrysanthemum
✔ Daffodil
✔ Delphinium
✔ Elephant Ear
✔ Philodendron
✔ Poinsettia
✔ Pothos
✔ Yew

mildly and take him back to the permitted area. Don't give in and relax the rules "just this once." After a while, your setter will learn to stay out of restricted areas.

You may also want to teach your English Setter to stay off the furniture. It will be less confusing if you make all furniture off-limits. When your puppy breaks the rules, pick him up, reprimand him, and place him on the floor. Repeat this procedure as many times as necessary. Your setter will soon learn that he belongs on the floor, not the furniture.

A new home can be an intimidating place when you're a newly adopted English Setter puppy.

The Play's the Thing

Puppies seem to think almost anything is a toy. You, however, may not appreciate your English Setter's creativity when he decides that your shoes, clothing, or furniture are his favorite playthings. Your puppy may also be putting himself in danger when he plays games like "Empty the Sewing Basket." To thwart these aggravating and potentially dangerous activities, you'll need to provide some toys made specifically for safe, dog- and owner-approved activities.

The average pet supply store has a vast array of dog toys, but they're mostly either chew toys or chase toys, with some overlap. Most other features, such as squeakers or cute shapes, are simply embellishments. Squeakers

TIP

Unsafe Toys

Some toys—even some marketed as dog toys—aren't safe for your setter. Don't let your pet play with anything that splinters, such as wood, plastic, and some kinds of bone; anything that can be swallowed, such as strings or toys with strings that can be chewed off, small balls, marbles, and other small objects; or anything that presents a strangling hazard, such as ropes and cords.

Before you turn your English Setter loose in your yard, make sure it's safe for your friend.

and bells can be dangerous if they can be dislodged and swallowed.

Rawhide or leather: Many dogs like items made of rawhide or leather. Rawhide bones, especially large ones, give a dog a lot of chewing exercise. The dog may swallow some of the rawhide as it softens up from extended chewing, but this doesn't seem to cause any problems.

Natural and synthetic bones: Your pet supply store probably also carries a variety of natural and synthetic bones for dogs. Some of these are beef leg bones that have been specially processed and smoked. Some are bones made of nylon that have been scented to smell like a real bone. Both of these products offer safe, bone-chewing satisfaction.

Balls: Dogs of all ages love balls. Choose one made of hard rubber, either solid or with thick enough walls, so it can't be torn open and chewed up. Make sure bells or squeakers are safely sealed inside. The ball should be large for your English Setter's mouth. A ball that's too small could be swallowed and cause a digestive tract obstruction. Dogs have also choked when a thrown ball became lodged in the throat, obstructing the windpipe. To avoid this, never throw a ball directly to your English Setter—roll it or throw it to one side.

Name, Rank, and Serial Number

Your English Setter should always wear some form of identification, even if he only goes outside in a fenced yard or on a leash. Dogs can escape from fenced yards; they can jerk the leash from their owner's hand.

Collars and Tags

Your setter's identification could be as simple as your phone number scratched on the metal plate of his collar. Some owners attach identification tags to the collar. Even a rabies immunization tag can help reunite a lost dog with its owner. These numbered tags list the veterinary clinic where the immunization was administered. Most clinics keep records of their tag numbers along with the owner's name. Tags are better than no identification at all, but collars and tags can be easily lost or removed. Because of this, tags provide little protection against dog theft.

Tattooing

Another method of canine identification is tattooing, which can be done by a veterinarian. Your phone number or other information can be tattooed on the inside of your English Setter's ear or on his abdomen. Tattooing offers more security against theft than collars and tags, but it does not provide absolute protection because tattooes can fade and alteration is possible.

Microchips

The most sophisticated canine identification system involves implantation of a microchip under the skin on the back of the neck. The microchip, about the size of a grain of rice, contains a number that can be read with a special scanner. The number, along with the owner's identification, is listed in a database maintained by the microchip manufacturer or another lost dog program, such as the AKC Companion Animal Recovery Program. Someone who finds a lost dog can't tell if the dog has a microchip or access the information, but many animal shelters and veterinary clinics have microchip reading devices. Implanted microchips are difficult to remove or alter, so they provide the best security against dog theft.

The Outside World

Your English Setter will enjoy being outdoors in nice weather, but you can't just shove him out the door—you've got to make sure he has a safe place to play. He'll need shade, shelter, and drinking water. Grass is cool and comfortable, but concrete surfaces are easier to clean and less likely to harbor fleas and ticks. If your English Setter's outside play area is hard-surfaced, be sure to provide some soft bedding, in case your pal wants to take a nap. Finally, the area should be adequately fenced. English Setters, especially the taller ones, need sizable fences—about 4½ to 5 feet (1.4–1.5 m) high, depending on your setter's size. It's better to have it too high at first, because once it's built, it's difficult to make a fence higher unless you replace the entire thing. If your setter tries to dig under the fence, you may need to use chicken wire or chain link to extend the fence 18 to 24 inches (46–61 cm) underground.

Make sure there are no exposed nails or other sharp objects in your English Setter's outside play area. Get rid of any ropes, cords, or strings; these are choking hazards and can be dangerous if chewed on and swallowed. Don't keep chemicals, pesticides, or fertilizers where your setter can get into them. Make sure the play area doesn't contain toxic plants, such as yew, castor bean, or oleander.

In addition to your English Setter's backyard exercise sessions, the two of you will probably want to go for walks together. It's a good idea to always have a leash on your setter during your walks. Your town may also have a leash law requiring dogs to be leashed when off the owner's property.

No Place Like Home

If your English Setter will be outdoors for extended periods, for instance, while you're at work, he'll need a doghouse. The house should be roomy enough so that your setter can stand up and turn around in it. It should be constructed of weather-impervious material and insulated for winter warmth.

Note: I don't recommend using a heat lamp in the dog house, because of the dangers of electrical shock, fire, and overheating.

If the door is placed at right angles to the length of the house, your canine pal will stay warmer. It's also convenient if the roof lifts off so you don't have to crawl inside the doghouse to clean it.

Place the doghouse in a shady, sheltered part of the yard, with the door facing south to shelter the dog from cold north winds of winter, yet allowing summer's southern breezes to enter the house. The house should be slightly elevated on a platform or runners, but not raised so high that cold air can circulate beneath the floor. Bed the house according to the weather: a soft blanket or pad for summer, heavier bedding for winter. Straw makes a soft, warm bed as long as you fill the doghouse about one-third to one-half full (the straw will settle). Baled straw can be stacked around the doghouse to provide extra insulation. You can also bed the house with heavy blankets or thick cedar shaving-filled pads.

Weather or Not

Cold Weather

A healthy adult dog can tolerate very cold weather, *as long as the dog has been acclimated to it and has adequate shelter.* If a dog is suddenly forced to sleep in the open when it's 40°F (4.4°C), he won't be very comfortable. On the other hand, if he's gradually gotten used to the cold, he'll easily tolerate very low temperatures as long as he has a dry doghouse that's properly insulated and bedded.

It's all right to keep your English Setter inside during cold weather; just don't continually move him back and forth from your heated house to the frigid weather outside. Dogs handled in this fashion have a lot more health problems than those spending most of their time in either one place or the other. If your English Setter must stay outside in cold weather, make sure his doghouse is insulated and warmly bedded. Don't forget to provide adequate water; licking snow or ice won't meet his needs and will make it harder for him to stay warm. A heat lamp, outside the doghouse, will keep his water from freezing. If you can't use either of these methods, give him fresh water several times a day. You'll also need to feed him more—the extra calories will help keep him warm.

Summer

In the summer, your attention will be focused on the problem of how to keep your English Setter cool. If he's been acclimated to the hot weather and has ample water and shade, he'll probably get along just fine. Even when it's very hot, dogs don't usually develop heatstroke unless they are forced to remain in

Always confine your English Setter to a crate or carrier while traveling in the car.

Riding in the Car

There are bound to be times when you and your English Setter will need—or want—to go somewhere in the car. The trip will be more pleasant if your setter is used to riding in a car before you go.

Make car rides part of your puppy's regular routine. Start with short rides, then gradually increase the duration. Don't give up if your English Setter doesn't seem to enjoy riding in the car at first. Some dogs take longer than others to get used to it.

Always, without exception, confine your English Setter in a carrier while he's in the car. It's dangerous for both of you if he's loose in the car while you're driving. Don't rely on someone else to hold him, as he could escape, with disastrous results.

Carsickness

Carsickness can be a problem for some dogs, especially puppies. Signs of carsickness include restlessness, whining, drooling, and vomiting. Understandably, dogs that get carsick don't usually enjoy car trips. If your setter is prone to carsickness, you may want to try a few things to improve the situation.

✔ Don't feed him just before a car trip.

✔ Take short, slow rides that don't include a lot of turns and hills.

✔ Talk to your puppy and reassure him during the ride; carsickness can be made worse by anxiety.

✔ Act happy. Try to convince him that a car ride is fun, not something to be dreaded.

an environment where they can't dissipate excess body heat, for instance, an automobile with closed windows. Unlike their owners, dogs seldom "overdo it" in hot weather; they'd rather just lie around in the shade. Of course, a dog that does overexert, either voluntarily or involuntarily, in hot weather may develop heatstroke, but this is relatively rare. Most dogs usually stop exercising when they get too hot (for more on heatstroke, see page 58). If your English Setter must stay outside in hot weather, make sure there's ample shade outside the doghouse throughout the day. Most dogs don't like to be in their doghouses when it's really hot. *Be sure to provide plenty of water.*

✔ When your English Setter tolerates short rides without carsickness, very slowly increase the duration of the trips. Most of the time, the tendency toward carsickness goes away as the puppy matures and becomes a more experienced passenger.

Right: Having a companion to play with may keep your puppy from becoming bored while you're away from home.

Below: English Setters love to run. To prevent injuries and other problems, keep your dog safely confined in a fenced yard or on a leash.

When you housebreak a puppy, you're training it, just as you would train it to sit or heel. Like any type of training, it will take a while for the puppy to learn what it's supposed to do. Housebreaking will go smoother if you make it as easy as possible for your English Setter to choose the correct behavior. It's also helpful if you take advantage of a basic instinct that all dogs possess—keeping their "den" or "nest" clean.

Tips to Make the Housebeaking Process Easier

1. Don't send your puppy outside; instead, take him outside to a place where he's relieved himself before, or where you want him to, and praise him when he does it again.

2. Remember that puppies usually need to eliminate right after eating and right after they wake up. Get in the habit of taking him out at those times.

3. Don't punish your puppy for housebreaking accidents. A mild reprimand is sufficient. There's no need to spank him, and there's never any need to "rub his nose in it"— that's cruel and it teaches the puppy absolutely nothing! Don't even bother to reprimand your puppy if you discover a pile or puddle after the fact. He won't understand why you're so upset—his mind just doesn't work that way.

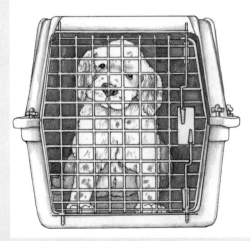

Confining your puppy to a carrier is an effective way of housebreaking. Dogs have a natural instinct to keep their "den" clean.

Age to Housebreak

It's usually easier to housebreak a puppy that's four to six months old. An older puppy is better able to control his bodily functions and has an easier time understanding what you expect. You can still take a younger puppy outside to relieve itself (remember to praise the correct behavior). Just don't expect too much and don't get upset about accidents.

Methods of Housebreaking

There are two methods of housebreaking. The direct method involves taking the puppy outside to relieve himself. This method is convenient for dog owners that have easy access to outdoors. It works best if the owner is frequently at home.

Dog owners who live in apartments or who are frequently away from home may want to use the second method of housebreaking, in which paper-training is used as an intermediate step toward the goal of outside elimination.

Direct Housebreaking

Before you start direct housebreaking, you'll need to get a crate or carrier for your

English Setter puppy. Choose one with plenty of space to turn around in. Line it with newspapers and some soft towels or a blanket for a bed. If possible, get a carrier that has a built-in holder for a water bowl or bottle, because your puppy will need water while he's in the crate. Make this indoor "doghouse" as comfortable as possible; you want your puppy to enjoy his time there.

With direct housebreaking, the puppy is taken outside frequently to relieve himself. Upon returning to the house, the puppy is confined to the carrier. You can also confine him in a space such as the kitchen or laundry room, if you can watch him closely, but a carrier works better. If your setter relieves himself inside, reprimand him mildly, then take him outside to the place he has used before. He'll quickly learn that it is inappropriate—and unpleasant, if he's confined to a carrier—to eliminate in the house.

Direct housebreaking using a crate or carrier is fast and efficient. Although the confinement may be difficult for both you and your puppy, it lasts for only a few weeks. That's not much time when you consider that some owners and dogs struggle through the housebreaking process for months or even years.

Paper-Training

If you decide to paper-train your English Setter puppy before teaching him to relieve himself outside, you'll need to select a tile-floored room, such as the kitchen or laundry room, in which to confine your puppy. Cover the entire floor of the room with several layers

Paper-training is a good way to housebreak a puppy if you must be away from home for extended periods of time.

of newspapers and confine your puppy in the room—remember to provide water. When he uses the papers, clean up the soiled papers and replace them. Keep doing this for a day or two, then leave one corner of the room bare. He'll probably ignore the bare spot and continue to use the papers. If he slips up and eliminates on the unpapered floor, don't overreact. Just reprimand him mildly (if you catch him in the act) and put him on the papers. When he consistently uses the papers, gradually enlarge the bare area until you have only about a 3-foot (91 cm) papered area. Let him use that area until you start taking him outside to relieve himself. At first, you'll need to take him outside frequently. When he learns that the appropriate place for elimination is outside, you can stop using the papers.

FEEDING YOUR ENGLISH SETTER

Mealtime is a major event in your English Setter's day, not because of the nutrients the food supplies, but because of the sheer joy of eating. You probably view the situation from a little different perspective. You want your English Setter to enjoy eating, of course, but you're more concerned that the food supplies all the nutrients your companion needs for optimal health.

Dog food companies spend millions of dollars developing products that provide complete nutrition and taste good too. Most dog owners can't come close to accomplishing this at home. And why bother? The work's been done already, and it's available at your grocery store. Just make sure you select a completely balanced food. It will say so on the label. Keep in mind that dogs of different ages have different nutritional needs.

Basic Nutrition

All dog foods contain a mixture of protein, carbohydrates, fat, vitamins, and minerals. How these components are combined determines the food's nutritional balance.

Tomatoes may be healthy for you to eat, but a balanced dog food is best for your English Setter.

Protein

Protein provides your English Setter with amino acids, the body's "building blocks." Amino acids are required for the growth and repair of body tissues, production of infection-fighting antibodies, and production of important enzymes and hormones. Protein is found in many foods, especially meat and dairy products. Protein must be consumed regularly because it cannot be stored in the body.

Carbohydrates

Carbohydrates, found in grains and other plant products, provide the fuel that powers the body for virtually every function from the smallest cells to the muscles used when your English Setter chases a ball. Excess carbohydrates are stored as glycogen in the liver or muscles or converted into fat.

Fat

Fat is also one of the body's principal fuels. It is essential for the production of certain hormones and is important in the functioning of some body systems, such as the nervous system. Vitamins A, D, E, and K are transported throughout the body in conjunction with fat molecules. Fat, which is readily stored in the body, is used as a back-up fuel when carbohydrates are unavailable. Stored body fat helps maintain body temperature in cold weather.

Vitamins

Vitamins are required for a variety of bodily functions. Nutritionally complete commercial dog foods contain all the necessary vitamins in the proper proportions, so supplementing your English Setter's diet with additional vitamins is not usually necessary. Excessive amounts of certain vitamins can actually be toxic to your dog. Providing vitamins beyond what your dog needs is also a waste of money, since the excess is simply excreted.

Minerals

Minerals, like vitamins, are involved in many bodily functions, including bone growth and healing, cellular metabolism, regulation of body fluid, and muscle and nerve function. Mineral supplementation isn't necessary if you feed your English Setter a good-quality balanced commercial food. Excessive mineral supplementation can have toxic effects.

Water

Water is an essential component of every function of your English Setter's body. Dogs can go for a long time without eating, but only a short while without water because the body cannot store water and

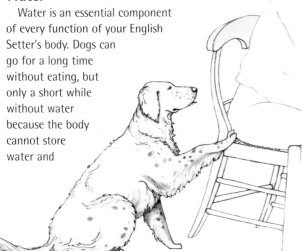

has only limited means for conserving it. Always provide your setter with an unlimited supply of fresh, clean water. Remember that water requirements increase during hot weather. In cold weather, make sure liquid water is readily available—dogs cannot take in adequate amounts of water by licking ice or eating snow.

Types of Food

Canned foods have the most moisture of the three forms of food; relished by most dogs, these products are often used to stimulate the appetite of a finicky eater or a dog recovering from an illness. Canned dog food is expensive, especially if you're feeding a large dog. It's easy to store, but the cans must be refrigerated after opening. Canned food shouldn't be used for free-choice feeding because it spoils rapidly at room temperature.

Semimoist dog food resembles ground meat and has a moisture content that is intermediate between dry and canned products. Because it requires no refrigeration after opening, semimoist food can be used for free-choice feeding. Unfortunately, these products contain high levels of sugars (sucrose and fructose) and preservatives. Because of this, semimoist foods are not recommended as a primary diet for most dogs.

It's hard to resist that sad, hungry face, but your English Setter will be better off eating food made just for dogs.

Dry food, which contains the least amount of water, is available in a variety of chunk sizes. Dry food is the least expensive type of dog food. It doesn't spoil when left in the food dish, unless moistened, so it can be used in a free-choice feeding program. Because dry food is bulky, it requires more storage space. It must be stored in a cool, dry, vermin-proof environment.

Feeding dry food without added water promotes healthy teeth and gums. It also helps satisfy a dog's chewing instinct. Dry food takes longer to eat, because it's bulkier and because it must be chewed at least a little before swallowing; this may contribute to a feeling of satiation. Dry food may not appeal to you, but most dogs like it well enough, particularly if it's been fed since puppyhood.

Switching Foods

If you want to switch your English Setter from canned or semimoist food to dry food, you'll probably have to do it "cold turkey," feeding only the dry food. At the regular mealtime, put a little dry food, perhaps moistened with some water, in the dog dish. If your dog won't eat, just leave the dish on the floor but don't leave it for more than an hour if you added water because it may spoil. Resist your English Setter's attempts to convince you that starvation is imminent unless you switch back to the favored food. Don't offer a different food or a between-meal snack. When it's mealtime, show your dog the dish again, or offer fresh water-moistened dry food. Don't worry if your setter doesn't eat—dogs can go for days without food; a healthy dog will not starve itself. Your setter will eat the dry food when she gets hungry enough. At this point, you may have to temporarily limit the amount you feed

and then gradually increase it as your dog's system becomes accustomed to the new diet.

Feeding Plans

Adult dogs are usually fed once or twice a day. Some people find that feeding twice a day decreases begging and scavenging. A once-a-day feeding can be given at any time as long as it's about the same time every day. Dogs that are fed in the evening are more likely to sleep at night. In all likelihood, your daily schedule will probably dictate your English Setter's feeding schedule.

Feed your setter in a quiet place away from the center of household activity. If your setter has a "den" in the house, you can place the food and water bowls nearby. It's all right to feed her outside as long as the feeding place is sheltered from inclimate weather and inaccessible to other dogs and bowl-robbing opossums and raccoons. Remember to provide fresh water at each location your English Setter frequents.

How Much to Feed

How much you should feed your setter depends on factors such as age and activity level. For basic guidelines, consult the dog food label for the manufacturer's recommendations. Healthy adult dogs should be fed just enough to maintain a normal weight, easily assessed on the basis of body condition. With your setter standing, stand behind her and place your thumbs on her spine so your fingers can move back and forth along the rib cage. You should be able to just feel the ribs. If you can't feel them at all, your setter's too fat; if you can easily feel every rib, your setter's too thin. If your English Setter loses weight on the

Puppies need food that's specially formulated to meet their nutritional needs.

manufacturer's recommended amount, increase the ration, increasing the number of feedings per day if necessary. If your English Setter starts to get a little pudgy, reduce the amount you feed.

Free-choice Feeding

With a free-choice feeding plan, the owner provides enough food to exceed the dog's daily requirement, allowing the dog to eat when and how much it wants. Free-choice feeding is the simplest feeding plan for the owner. Some dogs adjust readily to this plan, but others overeat

A healthy, balanced diet will keep your English Setter's coat soft and luxurious.

and become overweight. This plan makes it difficult to accurately determine daily intake. Free-choice feeding can be used in households with more than one dog, as long as multiple dishes are provided and an excess of food is always available.

Time-controlled Feeding

With a time-controlled feeding plan, the owner provides a surplus of food and the dog eats as much as it wants in a predetermined time.

Note: Most healthy adult dogs can eat enough food to meet their daily nutritional requirements in about 15 to 20 minutes.

Overeating with a time-controlled feeding plan is less of a problem than with the free-choice plan. It is also easier to determine whether the dog is eating.

Above: You and your English Setter will have a better relationship if you understand each other.

Left: Candy is not a healthy treat for your English Setter. Offer a dog biscuit instead.

Portion-controlled Feeding

With a portion-controlled feeding plan, the dog is offered a predetermined amount of food—the entire daily recommended ration in one feeding or half of the ration at each of two feedings—and eats it whenever it wants. This feeding plan works well for dogs that nibble, rather than gulp, their food. Portion-controlled feeding gives the dog owner the greatest amount of control with respect to quantity eaten. Alterations in food intake can be detected immediately.

Feeding No-Nos

We've talked a lot about what your English Setter should eat. Here are some things that she *shouldn't* eat:

1. Bones: Because they're brittle, chicken bones and pork chop bones can splinter and perforate the esophagus and other parts of the digestive tract. Ring-shaped round steak bones can get caught around your English Setter's lower jaw. Cooked bones, even large ones, become overly soft, allowing the dog to gnaw off excessive amounts, which can cause constipation. Let your English Setter safely satisfy her urge to chew with a nylon bone or rawhide chew.

2. Table food: If you're feeding a balanced dog food, your pet doesn't need table food. In addition to unbalancing her daily diet, it will decrease her appetite for dog food and could lead to obesity.

3. Alcohol: It's cruel and irresponsible to ever give a dog even a small amount of an alcoholic beverage. Dogs are extremely sensitive to the effects of alcohol; because most dogs are much smaller than humans, a small drink for a human can be dangerously toxic for a dog.

4. "Recreational" drugs: Like alcohol, these substances can have profound and disastrous effects on dogs.

5. Chocolate and other kinds of candy: Dogs don't need sweets and they don't need the dental problems that sweets cause. Besides, there may be more than tooth trouble lurking in that candy bar—chocolate contains theobromine, a substance that can be toxic to dogs. Give your English Setter a dog biscuit instead.

Dogs with Special Dietary Needs

Puppies, pregnant or nursing bitches, geriatric dogs, and dogs with certain health problems have nutritional requirements different from those of the average healthy adult dog.

Puppies

Puppies have a higher metabolic rate than adult dogs and require more calories per pound of body weight. Puppies also need more protein to provide for their rapid growth. These requirements can be met by feeding a balanced commercial puppy food. Dry food is recommended, although a small amount of water can be added for very young puppies. Starting puppies on dry food as soon as possible after weaning increases their acceptance of dry food. If you feed a nutritionally complete puppy food, there is no need to supplement the diet with additional meat, milk, eggs, or vitamins.

Young puppies that have just been weaned should be fed four times a day, because it's difficult for them to consume adequate amounts of nutrients when fed less frequently. When the puppy is about 10 to 12 weeks old, the number of feedings can be decreased to three a day. You'll need to increase the total daily intake of food as the puppy grows. Decrease the daily feedings to two a day when the puppy is about six months old. This feeding schedule can be maintained indefinitely or you can decrease to once-a-day feedings when your puppy is one year old.

Pregnant or Lactating Bitches

A bitch should be neither too fat nor too thin before she's bred. Early in the pregnancy, her regular diet of a good-quality commercial food should be sufficient. You'll need to feed her more food as her weight increases. As her intake increases, feed smaller amounts more frequently. If your English Setter mom-to-be is eating a good-quality, nutritionally complete dog food, she won't need additional supplements. She'll get all the nutrients she needs from her food.

Some bitches don't eat very much for a day or so after whelping. The new mother's appetite and nutritional requirements then increase dramatically, peaking about three weeks after whelping. During this time, the bitch should be fed as much as she wants to eat in small, frequent feedings. Don't be surprised if her food intake doubles or even triples in the first few weeks after whelping—lactation uses up a lot of calories! As during pregnancy, supplements are not needed during lactation.

When it's time to start weaning the puppies, restricting the bitch's food intake will help decrease her supply of milk. Some experts recommend decreasing the ration to prepregnancy levels. Others recommend a more drastic reduction: On the first day of weaning, withhold food completely, but always have water available, of course. On the second day, give her one-fourth of her normal (nonpregnant) maintenance diet. On the third day, give her one-half her maintenance diet. Increase this to three-fourths on the fourth day. After this, she can be returned to a regular (nonpregnant) maintenance diet.

Geriatric Dogs

Dogs, like people, tend to become less active as they age. To keep your older setter from becoming too fat, you'll need to decrease the amount of calories fed or increase your dog's activity. You might try feeding a reduced-calorie commercial food, which lets you limit your setter's caloric intake without decreasing the amount fed. As an alternative, a daily walk might keep the weight off without any dietary change at all.

Your older English Setter may not digest food as easily as she did when she was younger, so you may want to feed three smaller meals rather than one or two a day.

Older dogs are sometimes plagued with chronic health problems, such as heart disease or kidney disease. There are special diets for dogs with these and other conditions. Consult your veterinarian.

HEALTH CARE

The Healthy English Setter

The healthy English Setter presents an impressive and unforgettable picture. This athletic aristocrat is alert, responsive, and interested in everything. His soft, silky coat overlays supple skin that is free of bare patches and external parasites. His trim physique belies a hearty appetite; you can just feel the ribs when you run your hand across his side. When you look at his face, clear, bright eyes capture your attention. The tongue and gums are pink, the teeth are clean, and there's no tartar buildup or "doggy breath." All of this didn't just happen by accident. Rather, the healthy English Setter is the splendid result of a good genetic makeup combined with the best of care.

Your Veterinarian

For optimal health, your English Setter will need a lifetime of proper veterinary care. In addition to providing medical care, a veterinarian is a valuable source of information about behavior, breeding, and nutrition. Although you may be tempted to seek veterinary care and advice from neighbors, breeders, or pet shop personnel, or even just "do it yourself," take the time to find a veterinarian to provide for the health needs of your English Setter. There is simply no substitute for professional veterinary care administered by a veterinarian.

Sometimes, choosing a veterinarian is easy. There may be only one in your town or area. Some pet owners, however, especially those who live in metropolitan areas, may have to choose from many veterinarians, including various specialists. More and more veterinarians are limiting their practice to certain species—dogs and cats, for instance—or even a certain clinical specialty, such as surgery. You'll probably want to take your English Setter to a veterinarian who treats primarily dogs and cats.

So how do you find this veterinarian? Talk to your dog-owning friends. Find out which veterinarian they use. If there's a veterinary school nearby (there are 31 in North America), people there can probably give you the names of several veterinarians in your area.

It's a good idea to meet the veterinarian and see the clinic or hospital before your English Setter needs veterinary care. Most veterinarians will be happy to set up an appointment for a get-acquainted tour if you call ahead to arrange it. During the visit, observe how the veterinarian and staff get along with the patients (and owners), tour the clinic, and ask lots of questions. If you like what you see, you can go ahead and make an appointment for your English Setter if you need to. If you don't think this is the right choice, continue searching for a veterinarian and facility that you and your setter will be happy with.

Proper veterinary care can keep your English Setter feeling "on top of the world."

Immunizations

Proper immunization will protect your English Setter from many serious and possibly fatal diseases. The initial immunizations are usually administered singly or in series in the first four to six months of life, with booster immunizations at regular intervals after that. For maximum protection, puppies *must* receive the entire series of initial immunizations and adult dogs *must* receive their booster immunizations at the recommended intervals. Your veterinarian can recommend the best immunization schedule for your dog for the diseases discussed below.

Rabies

Rabies, a viral disease that can affect any mammal, is most commonly contracted when saliva from an infected animal enters an open wound, usually a bite wound. A rabid dog may first demonstrate an unusual behavior change: A previously shy dog may become friendly, or a good-natured dog may become nervous and reclusive. The second stage of rabies is characterized by excitability and hyperreactivity. The dog may become very aggressive and try to bite inanimate or even imaginary objects *(furious rabies)*. Sometimes this stage is very transient or even absent; instead the dog becomes stuporous and oblivious to its surroundings *(dumb rabies)*. In the final stage of rabies, the dog becomes progressively paralyzed. Drooling ("foaming at the mouth") occurs because paralysis of the jaw muscles makes swallowing difficult. Death usually occurs within 24 to 48 hours.

The first rabies immunization is usually administered at three to four months of age, with booster immunizations one year later and either annually or triennially after that. The reimmunization schedule depends on the type of vaccine and, in some areas, local law. Your veterinarian can tell you when your English Setter should be reimmunized.

Distemper

Canine distemper is a highly contagious viral disease spread primarily via body secretions. The virus may also be found on brushes, blankets, and food bowls. The incubation period for distemper is 14 to 18 days. Young, nonimmunized dogs are highly susceptible to the disease. A dog in the early stages of distemper may seem to have a mild cold with a slight fever, nasal discharge, and general malaise. As the disease progresses, the dog develops anorexia, vomiting, diarrhea, coughing, and a puslike discharge from the eyes and nose. The later stages of distemper are characterized by signs of encephalitis (inflammation of the brain)—seizures, muscle twitching, incoordination and/or circling, and blindness. The dog may act frightened and cry out as if in pain. Dogs that recover from distemper may have permanent neurologic problems, such as muscle spasms and impaired vision.

Puppies may not develop adequate protection when first immunized against distemper, because the antibodies they received from their mother interfere with their response to the vaccine. Because of this, puppies should receive multiple distemper immunizations between six and fourteen weeks of age. Puppies younger than 10 weeks of age are sometimes immunized with a combination distemper/measles vaccine. Because canine distemper virus is closely related to human measles virus, measles vaccine will induce immunity to distemper even in the presence of maternally derived antibodies. This immunity is temporary, however, and the puppy should receive regular distemper immunizations after the age of 10 weeks.

Hepatitis

Hepatitis is a viral disease most often seen in young dogs. Dogs contract hepatitis by inhaling or ingesting the virus, which is shed by an infected dog in all bodily secretions. The incubation period for hepatitis is four to seven days. Most infections are inapparent, but occasionally the virus causes a rapidly progressing, fatal disease that resembles distemper and parvovirus infection.

Initially, the dog with hepatitis may have a high fever—103 to 106°F (39–41°C) that decreases within 24 hours. With a mild infection, the dog may recover after a day or two. In moderate cases, the temperature decreases, then increases again after one or two days. The dog may be lethargic and refuse to eat. Abdominal tenderness may be present. Severe hepatitis causes tiny hemorrhages, especially on the gums, vomiting, bloody diarrhea, and abdominal tenderness and distension. Coughing may occur and sometimes progresses to pneumonia. Dogs with severe hepatitis may become comatose and die, or may die from shock.

The immunization schedule for hepatitis is essentially the same as for distemper.

Leptospirosis

Leptospirosis is caused by a spiral-shaped bacteria called a spirochete. The organism is shed in the urine. Infection occurs via direct contact with infected urine or by contact with contaminated substances.

Leptospirosis initially causes fever, vomiting, and anorexia. As the disease progresses, the dog may develop muscle soreness, bloody diarrhea, excessive thirst, excessive urination, and sores in the mouth. Jaundice may occur. Dogs that have recovered from leptospirosis may shed the organism for up to four years.

The immunization schedule for leptospirosis is the same as for distemper.

Parvovirus

Parvovirus infection causes disease of variable severity ranging from inapparent to rapidly fatal. Factors such as age, stress, intestinal parasites, or bacterial infection may predispose a dog to severe disease. The principal signs of parvovirus infection include vomiting, diarrhea, lethargy, and anorexia. In severe cases, persistent vomiting and severe bloody diarrhea may lead to death in less than 24 hours. Young puppies infected with parvovirus sometimes develop inflammation of the heart (myocarditis). A dog that has recovered from parvovirus infection will have lifelong immunity.

Puppies may not develop full immunity when first vaccinated against parvovirus infection, because the antibodies they received from their mother interfere with the response to immunization. Because of this, some veterinarians recommend parvovirus immunization every three weeks starting at six weeks of age and continuing until eighteen weeks of age. Parvovirus vaccine is sometimes given in conjunction with immunizations for distemper, hepatitis, and leptospirosis, with a fourth dose administered between 16 and 18 weeks of age. Immunity lasts for one to three years. Your veterinarian can recommend the best immunization schedule for your English Setter.

Kennel Cough

Kennel cough is commonly caused by the bacteria *Bordetella bronchiseptica*, but canine

These puppies need proper immunizations to protect them from serious diseases like distemper and rabies.

adenovirus and parainfluenza virus are also frequently involved.

Though highly contagious, kennel cough is usually a mild, self-limiting disease. Infected dogs have mild-to-severe recurrent coughing episodes that are aggravated by exercise, excitement, or pressure on the trachea (windpipe). Coughing episodes often end with gagging, which owners sometimes confuse with vomiting. Recovery takes about seven to ten days. Lower respiratory tract obstruction may develop, but pneumonia rarely occurs. However, nursing puppies that have kennel cough may die if their airways become clogged with thick mucus. Recovered dogs can shed infective organisms for more than three months. Some dogs become persistently infected carriers.

Immunization against kennel cough does not completely prevent infection, but decreases the incidence and severity of the disease. Puppies are usually immunized with intranasal vaccine before weaning.

Coronavirus

Canine coronavirus infection is a highly contagious viral disease of variable severity. Most infections in adult dogs are inapparent or mild. In clinically apparent infection, coronavirus causes diarrhea with or without vomiting. The stool has a characteristic orange color and is particularly foul-smelling. Death is uncommon in adult dogs, but the infection can be fatal in young puppies.

Coronavirus is spread through contact with the fecal material of infected dogs that can shed the virus for two weeks or more after infection. Because of this, the disease can spread rapidly in environments where there are large numbers of dogs, such as dog shows and kennels. Fortunately, coronavirus is quite susceptible to most commercial disinfectants and strict attention to hygiene will limit its spread.

Immunization against canine coronavirus provides only partial protection. Dogs frequently exposed to dogs from varied sources should be immunized. Immunization is also recommended if laboratory results indicate coronavirus is the cause of clinically apparent disease. Two immunizations are initially given three to four weeks apart, regardless of the dog's age.

Lyme Disease

Lyme disease is caused by *Borrelia burgdorferi*, which is carried by deer ticks. The disease causes a sudden onset of fever, weakness, joint pain, and lameness. Sometimes a characteristic "bull's-eye" rash—circular white central areas surrounded by red—appears at the site of an infective bite. The lameness may be transient and recur at variable intervals. Lyme disease can be treated with antibiotics. If left untreated, it can cause serious sequelae and even death.

The ticks that carry Lyme disease are found primarily on certain species of deer and mice. The infective organism is passed to the host when the tick feeds for 24 to 48 hours. The incidence of Lyme disease is highest in the Northeast (Massachusetts to Maryland), the upper Midwest (Wisconsin and Minnesota), and the West Coast (California and Oregon).

Effective tick control is an important factor in controlling exposure to Lyme disease (see page 63 for more on tick control).

Dog owners in Lyme disease areas may want to consider immunization for their dogs. The first Lyme disease vaccines provided only limited protection and were most effective in dogs that had not been previously exposed. Much more effective vaccines are now available. At least one provides immunity despite previous tick exposure and also combats existing Lyme disease infections.

Reimmunization (Boosters)

In the past, annual boosters were recommended for most of the commonly administered immunizations. This advice is currently being reconsidered, because information indicates that the protection derived from immunization of adult dogs can last for three years or more *for some diseases,* notably distemper, parvovirus, and rabies. Thus, future booster recommendations for these diseases may center around a three-year schedule. Some vaccines, such as those against parainfluenza virus, *Bordetella bronchiseptica,*

leptospirosis, and Lyme disease, do not provide protective immunity for even one year. Annual boosters may continue to be recommended for these diseases, with more frequent reimmunization advised for dogs at increased risk for exposure. Your veterinarian can recommend the best booster schedule for your English Setter.

Signs of Illness

Recognizing some of the more common signs of illness will help you decide when your English Setter needs veterinary care. Your accurate description of your dog's symptoms will also help your veterinarian make a diagnosis, since some of the symptoms you observe at home may not be readily apparent at the veterinary clinic if your setter is apprehensive or excited.

Vomiting: Isolated episodes of vomiting are usually not serious. If vomiting is persistent (more than two or three times in eight hours, especially if food and water have been withheld), or the vomit contains blood, consult your veterinarian.

Diarrhea: Like vomiting, isolated episodes of diarrhea are probably not cause for concern. Severe, persistent diarrhea, lasting more than 24 hours, with or without blood or mucus in the feces, should be reported to your veterinarian.

Fever: The normal canine body temperature is about 100.5 to 102.5°F (38–39.2°C). Excitement or vigorous activity can increase body temperature, so make sure your English Setter has been quiet for at least 20 minutes before taking his temperature.

Anorexia (not eating): A missed meal is probably nothing to worry about as long as your English Setter acts normal otherwise. If he's lethargic and depressed or has other signs of illness, such as vomiting or diarrhea, consult your veterinarian.

Excessive water consumption (polydipsia) and excessive urination (polyuria): Dogs normally drink a lot of water on a hot day. However, if your English Setter drinks excessive amounts of water even when the weather is not hot, you should consult your veterinarian, since this may indicate a serious illness such as diabetes or renal disease. Excessive urination often occurs with excessive water consumption and can be a sign of the same serious illnesses.

Abdominal pain: Abdominal pain occurs with many different conditions, including trauma, infections, intestinal obstructions, or foreign bodies. Consult your veterinarian promptly.

Bloody urine (hematuria), absence of urination (anuria): Hematuria may indicate that your English Setter has a bladder infection (cystitis), bladder stones (cystic calculi), or both. Report this symptom to your veterinarian. Sometimes, especially in male dogs, a bladder stone becomes lodged in the urethra (the tube that leads from the bladder to the exterior of the body), making urination impossible. This is an emergency situation requiring *immediate* veterinary care.

Weight loss: Your veterinarian should evaluate any weight loss that cannot be attributed to reduced food intake or increased activity. A number of disorders, such as internal parasites and diabetes, can cause unexplained weight loss.

Loss of consciousness: Loss of consciousness may occur with injuries, poisoning, seizures, or heart disease. Any loss of consciousness should be reported to your veterinarian immediately.

Seizures: Many conditions, including diseases such as epilepsy, and poisoning, can cause seizures. Any seizure should be reported to your veterinarian immediately.

Specific Health Problems

Cuts and Bleeding

Cuts (lacerations) range in severity from minor to life-threatening. Arterial bleeding, which is bright red spurting blood, is usually more serious than venous bleeding, which is dark flowing blood. To stop either venous or arterial bleeding, place a clean cloth directly on the wound and apply gentle but firm pressure. A tourniquet is not recommended because it can cause pain and tissue damage if not used correctly. Take your English Setter to your veterinarian if you cannot control the bleeding or you think the laceration may need sutures (stitches).

Footpad lacerations occur frequently in dogs. These cuts tend to bleed profusely. They are usually not sutured but often need to be bandaged to stop the bleeding and protect the wound.

Vomiting and Diarrhea

As mentioned previously, an isolated episode of vomiting is usually not cause for alarm. Many dogs vomit occasionally, especially after eating grass or a very large meal. Likewise, an isolated episode of diarrhea is not unusual, especially in nervous dogs or during hot weather when water consumption is increased. Repeated vomiting or diarrhea, however, may indicate a serious problem such as a gastrointestinal infection, foreign body, or obstruction. Electrolytes, essential components of many chemical reactions in the body, are lost during vomiting and diarrhea. Dehydration may also occur with repeated episodes. Young puppies are particularly prone to becoming dehydrated by persistent vomiting and diarrhea.

A dog with frequent vomiting and/or diarrhea should be examined by a veterinarian. If your English Setter is vomiting repeatedly, withhold food and water, because eating and drinking will usually cause more vomiting. If your dog seems thirsty, you may offer ice cubes or chips (ice is often better tolerated than water). If further vomiting occurs, discontinue the ice. Do not administer any medications unless directed to do so by your veterinarian.

Gastric Dilatation–Volvulus (Bloat)

Gastric dilatation-volvulus (GDV) is characterized by rapid and excessive accumulation of gas in the stomach (gastric dilatation), with subsequent twisting (volvulus). Large, deep-chested dogs are most frequently affected.

A dog with GDV is restless and uncomfortable. The abdomen is markedly distended, with a hollow, drumlike sound when tapped. The dog may attempt unsuccessfully to vomit. Signs of shock soon become evident if the GDV is left untreated.

A dog with GDV needs *immediate* veterinary care. Various measures may be required to treat the problem, ranging from uncomplicated stomach decompression, if only dilatation is present, to major surgery to correct a volvulus and prevent recurrence. Fluid therapy and medication are often needed to treat the shock that accompanies GDV.

Rapid consumption of large meals, especially dry or soy-based food, drinking large amounts of water after eating, and strenuous exercise after eating have been suggested as causes of GDV, but not conclusively proven. Nevertheless, modifying your English Setter's feeding schedule to two or three small feedings per day and restricting post-feeding water consumption and exercise may help prevent this disorder.

Fractures (Broken Bones)

A closed fracture, or simple fracture, is one with no open wound. An open fracture, or compound fracture, is one in which an open wound occurs. Open fractures are more serious because the wound increases the risk of infection.

You can't always tell just by looking if a dog has a fracture, especially if the fracture involves the foot, the ribs, or the head. A broken leg, however, may dangle oddly or appear to have an extra joint.

A dog with a fracture should be seen by a veterinarian as soon as possible. Do not attempt to bandage the injury. Move your English Setter gently and carefully to minimize movement of the broken bone. Remember that even gentle dogs sometimes react violently to pain; to avoid being bitten, you may need to muzzle your setter before handling him.

Eye Problems

English Setters, because of their love of coursing through rough terrain, are particularly susceptible to ocular (eye) foreign bodies, such as grass, plant seeds, grit, and splinters. The discomfort associated with foreign bodies depends on the location of the object, and whether or not it is embedded in the eye or surrounding structures. Tearing, squinting, or holding the lid tightly shut, and nervousness about being touched near the eye are signs of ocular pain. If you think your setter has an ocular foreign body, gently pry the lids apart and carefully examine the eye. You may need to get someone to hold your dog while you do this. If the eye is painful, you may need to muzzle your setter. Without touching the eye, gently flood it with warm water or eye-irrigating solution, such as Dacriose or Eye-Stream, available at your pharmacy, dripped from a cotton ball. Repeat as necessary. *Do not* try to remove the foreign body with a cotton swab, gauze pad, or tissue. If you cannot wash the object out of the eye, take your English Setter to your veterinarian as soon as possible.

Conjunctivitis is an inflammation of the lining of the eyelids (the conjunctiva), which may be caused by infection or contact with irritating substances. With conjunctivitis, the conjunctiva are reddened and the eye(s) may be held tightly shut. A mucous or puslike discharge may be present. Tearing may also occur.

Corneal injuries occur when the cornea, the clear outer covering of the eye, is scratched or punctured. These injuries are often extremely painful. Excessive tearing may occur and the dog may resist opening the eye. Sometimes the wound cannot be detected without special diagnostic techniques. In other cases, the cornea may appear cloudy over the injury.

A cataract is a cloudiness of the lens, located within the eyeball behind the iris (colored part). The cloudiness can sometimes be seen when you look directly into the dog's eyes. Severe cataracts can cause blindness. Sometimes vision can be at least partially restored by surgical removal of the affected lens. Many older dogs develop senile cataracts, but these are not considered as serious as cataracts in a younger dog and are not usually treated.

Glaucoma is a disease that causes excessive pressure within the eyeball. The increased pressure eventually damages the delicate structures of the eye, causing blindness. Glaucoma can sometimes be treated successfully with medication. In advanced cases, removal of the eye may be necessary.

All eye problems, with the possible exception of minor ocular foreign objects, should be evaluated by your veterinarian. Prompt treatment may save your English Setter's sight. Other than flooding the eye to remove minor foreign objects, you should never attempt any type of home treatment for an eye problem unless directed to do so by your veterinarian.

Ear Problems

The most common ear problem of dogs is otitis externa, or inflammation of the external ear canal. Otitis externa can be caused by bacterial, fungal, or yeast organisms, as well as embedded foreign objects such as foxtails or grass awns. The English Setter's long ears offer some protection from foreign bodies, but they also restrict air circulation to the external canal, increasing the likelihood of otitis externa from other causes. A dog with otitis externa may shake his head or scratch or paw at the ear. The affected

Good health care is essential for keeping your English Setter looking and feeling great.

ear may have a discharge and an odor. Veterinary attention is necessary for diagnosis and treatment of otitis externa. Left untreated, the infection/inflammation can spread to the middle ear (otitis media) or the inner ear (otitis interna). Dogs with otitis media or otitis interna often have balance problems (balance is governed primarily by the semicircular canals, which are located in the inner ear), characterized by head tilt, circling, and incoordination. In addition, a rhythmic usually side-to-side movement of the eyes called nystagmus may be evident. In rare cases, untreated otitis interna may cause erosion of the skull bones (osteomyelitis) or meningitis.

Heart Disease

Heart disease may be congenital (present at birth) or acquired (developed since birth). Congenital heart diseases are often characterized by structural abnormalities, such as defects between adjacent chambers of the heart. Some congenital abnormalities can be corrected surgically. Acquired heart disease takes many forms; the cause is not always known. A common acquired heart disease in dogs is mitral insufficiency, in which the valve between the left atrium and left ventricle does not close properly, allowing some of the blood to flow backward instead of forward. Mitral insufficiency can often be managed with medication.

A dog with heart disease may be lethargic and tire easily, especially during exercise. Breathing may be rapid or labored; a chronic cough may be present. In some cases, the abdomen becomes distended. These symptoms

Foreign objects in the eyes and ears can be a problem for English Setters that do a lot of hunting.

vary depending on the specific condition, as well as its severity.

Skin Problems

Skin problems have many causes, including external parasites (fleas, ticks, and mites), fungi, bacteria, and allergies. Alterations in the skin and/or haircoat can also occur with certain endocrine diseases, such as Cushing's disease. Depending on the condition, the skin may be dry and scaly or moist and oozing. The problem may be generalized or localized. Skin problems often cause itching. Scratching leads to skin abrasions and secondary bacterial infections. Hair loss (alopecia) may occur in limited patches or all over the body. Because of the diversity of skin problems, proper veterinary care is essential for identifying the cause and instituting effective treatment.

Cancer

Cancer is a significant cause of illness and death in dogs, particularly those older than 10 years of age. Cancer can take many forms. Some cancers appear as lumps on the body or as sores that don't heal, while others cannot be visualized without the use of special diagnostic techniques. Sometimes, cancer causes symptoms that mimic another disease.

The prognosis for a dog with cancer varies, depending on the type of cancer, the size of the tumor(s), the duration of illness, whether it has spread to other parts of the body, and the treatment. Substantial progress has been made in cancer treatment for animals. Surgery, chemotherapy, and radiation therapy are often combined.

Poisoning

Substances that are poisonous to your English Setter range from seemingly innocuous compounds such as chocolate to more obvious poisons such as strychnine. Although most poisoning occurs when the dog eats a toxic substance, poisoning can also occur via skin contact or inhalation.

Symptoms of poisoning vary considerably. Vomiting may occur with some poisons, but not others. Some poisoned dogs are lethargic or even comatose; others are restless or agitated. Progressively severe seizures may occur with some poisons. In most cases, the symptoms are dependent on both the toxic substance and the degree of exposure.

Any suspected poisoning should be reported to your veterinarian immediately. If you know what your dog has been exposed to, relate this information, as well as any label or container information (if available).

Heatstroke

Heatstroke occurs when a dog cannot rid itself of excess body heat. Factors that predispose a dog to heatstroke include a heavy haircoat, excessive activity, and confinement in a poorly ventilated, warm environment.

Perhaps the most common and most easily preventable cause of heatstroke in dogs is confinement in a car on a warm day. *Never* leave a dog in a closed car or even one with the windows partly rolled down, even on a mild day. The temperature inside the car can quickly become dangerously high.

A dog with heatstroke is usually lethargic and has an extremely high body temperature. Signs of shock may be present. Since heatstroke can be fatal, immediate veterinary care is necessary. Emergency procedures to help lower body temperature include wetting the fur with cool, not cold, water, placing washcloth-wrapped ice packs in the groin area, and offering cold water or ice chips, if the dog is conscious.

Shock

Shock is a state of circulatory collapse, which can be caused by trauma, severe infection, cardiac disease, or poisoning. The dog in shock is usually depressed and listless. The gums are often pale and may feel cool to the touch. The heart rate and respiratory rate are usually rapid.

A dog in shock needs immediate veterinary care. Cover your English Setter with a blanket and keep him as quiet as possible. Do not administer food, water, or any medication unless directed to do so by your veterinarian.

Hip Dysplasia

Hip dysplasia is an inherited abnormality of the hip joints causing variable degrees of arthritic changes and lameness. Puppies whose parents are free from hip dysplasia are less likely to have it, but this is not guaranteed. Hip dysplasia is diagnosed by radiographic evaluation. The Orthopedic Foundation for Animals (OFA) and PennHip currently certify the hip status of dogs. Hip dysplasia often causes progressively worsening arthritic changes in the hip joints; many dysplastic dogs eventually require medication to alleviate the pain associated with the disorder. Surgical procedures may be recommended for severely afflicted dogs. Dysplastic dogs should not be bred.

Elbow Dysplasia

Elbow dysplasia is an inherited abnormality of the elbow joint. The disorder causes arthritic changes in the joint and variable degrees of forelimb lameness. As with hip dysplasia, elbow dysplasia is diagnosed by radiographic evaluation. Certification of elbow status can be obtained through the OFA. Some dogs with elbow dysplasia require pain medication. Because elbow dysplasia is inherited, afflicted dogs should not be used for breeding.

Congenital Deafness

The incidence of congenital deafness in English Setters may be as high as 10 percent, according to some research studies. Some dogs are deaf in both ears (bilateral deafness), while others are deaf in only one ear (unilateral deafness). Congenital deafness can be diagnosed in puppies older than five weeks of age by a brainstem auditory evoked response (BAER) test. Dogs with unilateral deafness are suitable for pets; some are even shown, field-trialed, or hunted. Bilaterally deaf dogs require special care and training techniques to compensate for their total lack of hearing. Because this condition is inherited, afflicted dogs should not be bred, regardless of whether the deafness is in one or both ears.

Internal Parasites

Roundworms

Roundworms (ascarids) are the most common internal parasite of dogs. Dogs of all ages can become infected by ingesting embryonated eggs found mainly in the soil. In puppies, the ingested roundworm larvae first migrate to the lungs, where they are coughed up and swallowed. The larvae then pass into the small intestine, where they develop into adults. In older dogs, the ingested larvae migrate to other tissues, such as the muscles, kidneys, eyes, or brain, and become dormant. In females, the dormant larvae become active again during pregnancy and migrate to the placenta or mammary glands to infect the puppies. Because of this dormancy and reactivation cycle, virtually all puppies in North America are either born infected with roundworms or become infected when they nurse.

Symptoms: Heavy roundworm infection in young puppies may cause abdominal pain and distension, diarrhea, stunted growth, and dull haircoat. Larval migration through the lungs may cause pneumonia. Roundworm infection in adult dogs is usually asymptomatic.

Roundworm eggs can survive for months or years in soil. Roundworm-infested puppies are considered public health problems, because migrating roundworm larvae can invade the internal organs of humans, especially children (toxocaral visceral larval migrans).

Treatment: Because medication for round-worm infestation is usually quite safe, it can be administered to puppies as young as two weeks of age. Multiple treatments are often required to completely eliminate the parasites. Effective roundworm control in adult dogs, especially breeding females, and in the environment sub-stantially decreases the severity of infestations in young puppies.

Hookworms

Hookworms are bloodsucking intestinal parasites found in dogs of all ages. Infection most commonly occurs when infective larvae are ingested or penetrate the skin. Puppies can become infected prior to birth or while nursing, if the mother has hookworm larvae migrating within her body. Hookworms develop rapidly in the body and eggs are passed in the feces after two to three weeks.

Flowers are pretty to look at, but they could be dangerous if your English Setter decides to taste them.

The eggs hatch into infective larvae that can survive for three to four months under warm, moist conditions.

Symptoms: The clinical signs of hookworm infection, which are directly related to blood loss, include diarrhea, which may be tarry or bloody, pale gums, anemia, weakness, and ema-ciation. Blood transfusion may be required in severe cases, particularly in puppies.

Treatment: Treatment for both mothers and puppies is recommended in areas where hook-worms are a problem. Puppies can be treated as young as two weeks of age. As with most intestinal parasites, hookworm control is facili-tated by good sanitation and the use of imper-vious flooring in kennels and runs.

Whipworms

Whipworms are commonly found in the colon and cecum of dogs of all ages. Infection occurs when infective eggs are ingested. Whipworm infection is usually asymptomatic, but sometimes causes chronic or intermittent diarrhea. Because female whipworms shed eggs intermittently, several fecal examinations may be needed to diagnose whipworm infection.

Tapeworms

The life cycle of the tapeworm requires an intermediate host, usually fleas and lice, although one species of tapeworm is carried by rodents, rabbits, sheep, and cattle. Infection in dogs occurs when infected intermediate hosts are ingested.

Symptoms: Tapeworm infection is usually asymptomatic. The adult tapeworm is a long, flat parasite. The body is divided into rice-sized segments, called proglottids, which are shed in the feces. Proglottids are very motile and are often seen in the anal area or feces of infected dogs.

Treatment: Treatment for tapeworm infection involves eliminating both the parasites and the intermediate hosts. Thus, flea and lice control and elimination of scavenging and hunting are important aspects of effective treatment.

Coccidia

The term *coccidia* does not refer to a single parasite, but rather to any of a group of six protozoan parasites. Dogs are infected when they ingest infective oocysts (egg packets) or infective cyst-containing tissues of transport hosts, such as rodents and other prey.

Symptoms: Coccidia infection is usually asymptomatic, especially in healthy adult dogs.

Puppies kept in stressful, unclean, and overcrowded conditions are more likely to develop clinical disease. Malnutrition and concurrent disease may predispose a dog to clinical disease from coccidia.

Diarrhea is the predominant clinical sign of coccidiosis, but vomiting, lethargy, weight loss, and dehydration may also occur. If clinical signs are present, treatment is indicated, especially in newborn puppies.

Heartworms

Heartworms are mosquito-spread parasites that occur throughout the United States. The female mosquito ingests immature infective heartworms (microfilariae) during a blood meal on an infected dog. The microfilariae develop within the mosquito and are then introduced into the bloodstream of another dog when the mosquito feeds. After a three-month migration through the dog's body, the young adult heartworms enter the blood vessels and travel to arteries within the lungs. There they mature and begin producing microfilariae. The entire cycle takes about six months. Initially, adult heartworms are found only in the vessels of the lungs, but as their numbers increase, they eventually invade the vessels leading into the heart and the heart itself.

Symptoms: Many cases of heartworm infection are asymptomatic, but coughing, shortness of breath, and exercise intolerance may occur, especially in dogs with heavy infections. Heart failure may develop in severe cases.

Treatment: The usual treatment for heartworm disease is twofold: One drug is administered to kill the adult heartworms, and another to kill the microfilariae. Treatment is not without risk to the dog.

It is much easier to prevent heartworm disease than to cure it once it has developed. Monthly treatment with ivermectin or milbemycin oxime will prevent infection. Your English Setter should be tested for heartworms before starting a preventive medication program, because some preventive medication may cause serious reactions in heartworm-infested dogs. Heartworm preventive is administered year-round in warm climates, but is usually stopped during winter months in seasonal areas. Your veterinarian can recommend the best schedule for preventive medication. Dogs taking heartworm preventive medication should be retested for heartworms yearly (every six months in high-incidence areas), usually prior to resumption of preventive medication in areas where it is not administered year-round.

External Parasites

Fleas

Fleas are the most common parasite of dogs. These wingless bloodsuckers can jump great distances and move easily from dog-to-dog or from the environment onto a dog.

Fleas torment dogs in many ways. Their feeding and movement cause localized itching and inflammation. Some dogs become allergic to flea saliva and develop generalized dermatitis, called *flea allergy dermatitis.* Severely infested dogs, especially puppies or older dogs with concurrent disease, may become anemic due to chronic blood loss.

Symptoms: Fleas may be difficult to see on your English Setter. Signs of infestation include scratching, chewing at the skin, skin rash, and the presence of flea excrement—dark, reddish brown material that looks like dirt specks—on the skin. The English Setter's predominantly white coat makes it a little easier to detect the evidence of flea infestation. Look for fleas or their evidence at the base of the tail and the nape of the neck. The abdomen is also a good place to check, since the hair is usually sparser there.

Treatment: Flea control is difficult, because fleas can survive for a long time in the environment. Both the fleas on the dog and the fleas in the dog's environment must be eliminated. Your home's interior should be treated if your flea-infested dog has been inside, because fleas frequently live in furniture and carpets.

Flea collars, shampoos, dips, sprays, and powders have all been used, with variable results, to control fleas on dogs. Some of the newer flea control products are once-a-month oral medications, while others ("spot-ons" or "drop-ons") are applied locally to the skin once a month. Ask your veterinarian to recommend a flea control regimen for your English Setter. A professional exterminator may be needed to eliminate fleas in your home.

Ticks

Ticks are bloodsucking parasites that cause discomfort and transmit a number of serious diseases to both animals and humans.

Female ticks feed on the dog, become engorged, breed, and drop off to lay their eggs, after which they die. A single female may lay thousands of eggs. Male ticks remain attached to the dog for longer periods. After hatching, the larval ticks ("seed ticks") attach themselves to grass and foliage and wait for a passing host, such as dogs, other animals, or humans. After several stages of engorgement and molting, the larvae become adults and the cycle is repeated.

Removing a tick: Removing a tick from your English Setter is not difficult. After spraying the tick with tick spray (killing it loosens the mouthparts), grasp it close to the skin and slowly pull it off. You can use tweezers, if you choose. It's desirable to remove the entire tick, but sometimes part of the head remains embedded and causes a localized infection. Don't worry if this happens; these infections are usually self-limiting. After the tick has been removed, wash the area with mild antiseptic soap. Swabbing the area with alcohol either before or after tick removal is not recommended, because the alcohol will cause stinging and irritation. Ticks embedded in sensitive areas, such as near the eyes or in the ears, may need to be removed by your veterinarian.

Diseases carried by ticks: Ticks are notorious disease carriers. The American dog tick transmits diseases such as Rocky Mountain Spotted Fever, St. Louis Encephalitis, and tularemia to humans. This tick can also cause tick paralysis in dogs, cats, and humans. Tick paralysis occurs when toxins in the female tick's saliva are injected into the bite wound during feeding. Paralysis may result from the bite of just one tick, especially if the bite occurs on or near the head. The affected dog initially shows only rear quarter incoordination, but complete paralysis develops rapidly and spreads forward. Paralysis of the respiratory muscles can cause death. Removal of the offending tick(s) usually results in rapid recovery. Tick paralysis can be prevented by prompt tick removal, since it takes at least four days of feeding for signs of paralysis to develop.

The lone star tick also causes tick paralysis and transmits Rocky Mountain Spotted Fever.

Deer ticks transmit Lyme disease, a serious disease that can afflict both humans and dogs.

These pinhead-sized ticks are difficult to detect, so an effective continuous tick control program is very important for preventing Lyme disease. Deer ticks must be attached for at least 24 hours for transmission of the infective organism to occur. Substantial advances in the efficacy of Lyme disease vaccines have been made in recent years. Dog owners living in endemic areas should consult their veterinarian about vaccination for their dogs.

Tick control: Ticks are difficult to control. Effective control regimens involve treatment of the dog and the dog's environment, especially kennels and yards. In some cases, the interior of your house may need to be treated. Some of the newer flea control products also control ticks, but for a shorter time in some cases. Some tick control products contain chemicals that can be toxic to your dog, especially if several products are used concurrently. Always consult your veterinarian before applying any product to your dog or his surroundings. A professional exterminator may be needed to rid your yard and/or home of ticks. Repeat treatments are often necessary, especially during warmer weather.

Mites

Demodex canis is a tiny parasite that lives in the hair follicles and sebaceous glands of the skin. Although these mites can be found on normal dogs without signs of disease, factors such as youth, poor condition, short hair, and concurrent disease predispose some dogs to overt infection (mange). *Demodex* mites cause *red mange*, the most common form of mange in dogs, named for the chronic inflammation that leads to hair loss and thickening, wrinkling, and scaling of the skin. Secondary bacterial infections often occur and cause further inflammation and pustule formation.

Sarcoptes scabiei, a less common type of mite, causes sarcoptic mange, or scabies. These parasites burrow into the skin, causing intense irritation and itching. Dried blood and serum encrust the inflamed skin, which eventually becomes wrinkled and thickened. Hair loss is widespread.

Diagnosis: Your veterinarian can diagnose demodectic or sarcoptic mange with a skin scraping, a microscopic examination of cells and debris scraped from the skin.

Treatment: Your veterinarian can also prescribe appropriate treatment for either of these conditions. People can contract sarcoptic mange from dogs, but this is a relatively rare, and self-limiting, occurrence.

Ear mites live in the external ear canal, where they cause intense itching. A dog with ear mites may abrade the skin of its head and ears by scratching or rubbing. Head shaking may cause an aural hematoma, rupture of small blood vessels in the earflap with blood accumulation between the cartilage and skin. Ear mites cause the earwax to darken, so the ear appears to have dirt or dried blood inside it. The infection is diagnosed by observing the ear mites during an otoscopic examination. Your veterinarian can prescribe appropriate treatment. Usually all dogs and cats of the household are treated, because ear mites are readily spread from animal to animal.

Dental Care

Proper dental care is important for your English Setter's health. Dogs don't develop cavities as often as humans do, but they are quite susceptible to periodontal disease—gingivitis, periodontitis, and periodontal abcesseses. Gingivitis (inflammation of the gums) is usually caused by plaque, a soft, colorless scum that coats the teeth. Calculus, which is hard yellowish or brown deposits found on the teeth, facilitates plaque formation. Chronic gingivitis can lead to periodontitis and periodontal abscesses that cause destruction of the supporting structures holding the teeth in place. When these supporting structures are destroyed, the tooth is lost. The proliferation of bacteria in chronic periodontal disease can also lead to septicemia (bacteria in the bloodstream), which can produce a life-threatening infection of the heart valves called endocarditis.

Feeding your English Setter dry dog food and providing resilient chew toys, such as nylon bones, etc., will enhance the natural self-cleaning properties of the teeth. Regular brushing with a soft-bristled toothbrush and a palatable canine toothpaste will help prevent plaque formation. Regular cleaning of the teeth by your veterinarian will remove calculus and make at-home brushing more effective. At the time of cleaning, your veterinarian will also check for loose teeth, gingivitis, and other signs of periodontal disease.

Euthanasia

Saying good-bye is the most difficult aspect of pet ownership. It is especially painful if you must make the decision to end your dog's life. Hopefully, you will never have to make this decision, but even the best possible care cannot guarantee that your English Setter will live to old age and die a natural death. There are still diseases that are incurable, injuries that

The lush green grass could be hiding fleas and ticks. Make sure your English Setter is protected against these annoying and sometimes dangerous blood-suckers.

will not heal. Sometimes dogs with these conditions are able to live relatively normal lives for variable periods of time. In other cases, prolonging life means prolonging needless pain and suffering.

There is no simple way to make the decision about euthanasia. It's natural to resist the idea of euthanasia because of the grief you will experience. Don't ignore your feelings, but consider first the well-being of your English Setter. Try to remember that you would undoubtedly

grieve if your beloved companion were to suffer and slowly die from an incurable illness or injury.

When a dog is euthanized or "put to sleep," it is given an injection of a drug that acts like a very strong anesthetic. When the drug is injected, the dog first loses consciousness and then dies quickly and painlessly. Some owners want to stay with their dogs while euthanasia is performed, but it can be very upsetting to watch your pet die, even if you know there is no other choice. For this reason, many owners choose to say their good-byes and then leave the room. The decision is yours; do whatever you feel is most comforting for you and your dog.

If your English Setter has been hospitalized for illness, injury, and/or surgery, you may need to provide some nursing care when the patient returns home.

Restraint

Your English Setter may need to be restrained for certain treatments. Some dogs respond well to words, while others must be muzzled and held by an assistant. Always use the least amount needed to complete the task. Reassure your setter continually when any type of restraint is used.

Your nursing chores will be easier if someone holds your English Setter for you. The assistant should kneel next to the dog and place one arm over the dog's back, bringing the hand around to the dog's chest. The other hand is brought under his head to cup his cheek and skull area, on the side away from the assistant's body, and hold the dog's head close to the assistant's body. Because even a gentle dog can bite when stressed or in pain, the assistant should keep the dog's head as low as possible to avoid being bitten in the face.

If muzzling is necessary, you can use a purchased muzzle or you can make one.

✔ Take a 30-inch (76 cm) length of 2-inch (5 cm) gauze, or any soft, strong material, and make a loop by tying a loose half-hitch (overhand knot) in the center of it.

✔ Holding the ends, guide the loop, with the knot on top, over your dog's nose and pull the loop very tight. Bring the gauze ends under the lower jaw and tie another tight half-hitch.

✔ Bring the ends behind your setter's head and tie them in a bow (it's easy to untie). Make sure all of your ties are very tight; if they aren't, the muzzle won't work.

Taking Your English Setter's Temperature

Normal canine body temperature ranges from 100.5 to 102.5°F (38–39.2°C). You can use a glass rectal thermometer to take your English Setter's temperature, but digital thermometers are safer and easier to use. If you use a glass thermometer, shake it down to about 97°F (36.1°C) and place a dab of K-Y Jelly or petroleum jelly on the end. Gently insert it about 2 inches (5 cm) into the rectum. Hold onto the thermometer—it's easier if you hold your dog's tail and the thermometer together—and leave it in place for two to three minutes. For a digital thermometer, place a bit of lubricant on the tip, insert into the rectum, and hold it in place until the temperature has been recorded, usually a matter of seconds.

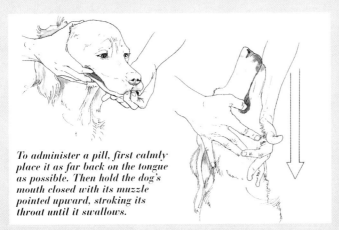

To administer a pill, first calmly place it as far back on the tongue as possible. Then hold the dog's mouth closed with its muzzle pointed upward, stroking its throat until it swallows.

Giving Medication

Oral medication: An easy way to give your English Setter a pill is to place it in a small ball of canned dog food or a piece of soft cheese and offer it as a treat. This method usually works if the dog has a normal appetite. If the "treat" is refused, however, you'll have to use another approach.

✔ Kneel or stand at your dog's side and bring your left hand (if you're right-handed) up over his head to grasp his muzzle.

✔ Place your other hand, which is holding the pill, on the lower jaw and gently tilt your English Setter's head straight up. This usually causes the mouth to open slightly.

✔ Open the mouth widely, then quickly place the pill as far back on the tongue as possible.

✔ Close your setter's mouth, hold it shut and rub his throat. After about a minute, let him open his mouth. If he spits the pill out, try again.

You don't have to open your dog's mouth to give liquids. Put the liquid in an oral dose syringe or large plastic eyedropper. Tilt your setter's head up a bit, insert the syringe or dropper in the corner of his mouth and dribble the liquid in.

Eye medication: Eye medication is usually in ointment or drop form. With either, it's important to avoid touching the eye with the applicator or your fingers. Most dogs tolerate ointment better than eyedrops.

To apply ointment, gently pull the lower eyelid down and deposit the ointment inside it. Hold the tube of ointment parallel to the eye's surface so there's less chance of injury if your setter moves suddenly. Close the eyelids with your fingers to distribute the ointment.

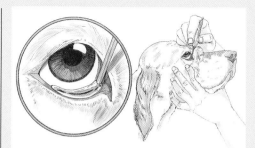

When administering eye ointment, be sure to hold the tube parallel to the surface of the eye. That way, if your English Setter moves suddenly, there's less likelihood of injury.

To apply drops, tilt your English Setter's head up, carefully hold the eyelids apart, and deposit the drops in the inside corner of the eye or into the lower eyelid. Hold the dropper close to the eye—you're less likely to miss your target and it's more comfortable for your dog.

Ear medication: Medicating a dog's ears is usually easy. Tilt your English Setter's head so the affected ear is up, gently pull the earflap up, and apply the medication into the ear canal. Make sure you hold the head securely immediately after medicating, because he may shake his head. Massage the ear to distribute the medication.

Topical medication: Topical (skin) medication may be ointment or liquid. Ointment can be applied directly or you can use your finger to apply it. Drops are usually applied directly to the skin. After applying either type, rub it in well, unless otherwise instructed by your veterinarian. The biggest problem with topical medication is keeping the dog from licking it off. Taking your English Setter for a walk or playing with him may distract him, so that he loses interest in the medication.

GROOMING YOUR ENGLISH SETTER

Keeping your English Setter looking great is going to take some work. The good news is that most grooming chores aren't too difficult, especially if you do a little each day. And the time you spend grooming your setter can be enjoyable for both of you.

Right from the Start

When your English Setter is a puppy, start getting her used to grooming routines. Acclimate her to brushing by using a soft brush for brief, but frequent, periods of brushing. Praise her when she sits still. Wipe her eyes, swab her ear leathers, handle her paws. If she gets nervous, stop and reassure her, then go back to what you were doing. Praise her when she allows you to continue. Repeat these lessons until your puppy will quietly let you perform all the necessary grooming chores except bathing, which she probably won't need until she's at least six months old.

Coat Care

Regular brushing will help keep your setter's coat and skin healthy. Start out by brushing her gently with a slicker brush or a stiff bristle

Regular brushing will keep your English Setter's coat and skin healthy.

brush, then use a metal comb to remove any dead hairs. Matted hair should be gently teased apart and combed out, if possible. Mats that can't be teased apart can usually be removed by carefully cutting lengthwise through the mat, in several places, if necessary, then combing until the mat is removed. Always cut lengthwise, *away* from the body, and work slowly and gently. If your English Setter's coat is badly matted, you may need to have a professional groomer remove them. Removal of large mats might require substantial clipping.

Bathing

Your English Setter will probably need to be bathed only every six to eight weeks, or even less frequently, depending on her activities and your tolerance for "doggy odor." Of course, some situations demand immediate attention, such as close encounters with tar, paint, mud, or—every owner's nightmare—a skunk!

To bathe your setter, you'll need a stiff bristle or slicker brush, dog shampoo, a sponge, cotton balls, bland eye ointment, and lots of towels. If it's a warm day, you can bathe your English Setter outside, but it may be easier to bathe her inside in a bathtub equipped with a nonskid surface or rubber mat.

✔ Before the bath, brush your setter with the bristle or slicker brush, carefully removing any mats, burrs or sticks from the coat. Pay close attention to the ears, the "feathers" (the long fringelike hair on the back of the legs, abdomen, and tail), and the spaces between the toes. If your setter has gotten into tar or paint, you may need to cut out the affected hair. Never use turpentine, kerosene, or gasoline to remove tar or paint from the coat. If you don't want to cut the coat, liberally apply vegetable or mineral oil to the affected area, then shampoo thoroughly 24 hours later.

✔ Place small cotton balls in your English Setter's ears to prevent water and shampoo from getting in them. Protect her eyes by applying a small amount of bland eye ointment to each.

✔ Adjust the water flow and temperature before you put your setter in the tub. The temperature should be comfortably warm. Check the water frequently to make sure the temperature stays comfortable.

✔ Now place your English Setter in the tub. Once she's settled down a bit, thoroughly wet her coat. Apply some shampoo with the sponge and work up a lather. Massage the lather all over your dog. Rinse thoroughly; a spray hose helps, but a pan or other container can also be used. Repeat the shampooing and rinsing. Squeeze the excess water out of the coat.

✔ Now you've got to get that big wet setter out of the tub and into a towel before she shakes water all over you and the bathroom! If you're quick, you can throw a towel over her and dry her off a little. Or, you can pull the shower curtain around the tub and let her shake away. This method works well as long as she doesn't immediately jump out of the tub, shake, and soak the bathroom anyway!

✔ After towel-drying your setter, you can finish drying her with a hair dryer set on "warm" or let her air-dry if it's a warm day. Air-drying works best if you can confine your English Setter so she won't run outside and undo all your work.

CHECKLIST

Grooming Supplies

✔ slicker brush or soft bristle brush
✔ metal comb
✔ dog shampoo
✔ sponge
✔ cotton balls
✔ bland eye ointment
✔ spray hose or pan for rinsing
✔ bathtub with a nonskid surface or rubber mat
✔ towels
✔ nail clippers

Ear Care

Your English Setter's ears don't need lots of elaborate care. Occasionally swab them with a finger wrapped in a soft cloth, and regularly check them for foreign objects, such as burrs or grass awns, or evidence of infection (otitis) or ear mites. Don't swab your dog's ears out with cotton swabs and don't use irritating substances such as alcohol on or in the ear. Consult your veterinarian if you detect any unusual odors or discharges. If you spot a foreign object in the ear canal, don't try to remove it as you could injure your dog's ear or drive the object farther into the ear. Let your veterinarian take care of this procedure.

Nail Trimming

Many dogs need to have their nails trimmed every four to six weeks, but this varies. Check your English Setter's nails weekly to make sure they aren't getting too long.

It helps to have someone assist you with nail trimming, especially if both you and your setter are inexperienced with it.

✔ Have your assistant hold your dog and talk to her.

✔ Grasp the paw and spread the toes. If the toenails are white, you'll see the pinkish *quick* in the center of the nail. Avoid cutting the quick, as it hurts and the nail will bleed. You can't see the quick in black toenails, so just nip off the tip.

✔ Continue until every nail has been trimmed; don't forget the dewclaws if present.

If you clip a nail too short, your setter will undoubtedly make a fuss. The nail will probably bleed more than you might expect, partly because the vessel has no soft tissue around it, but mostly because your setter will scramble around a lot and make the toenail bleed more. The bleeding isn't serious, just messy. You can

If your English Setter has black nails, trim just the tips to avoid cutting the quick. On white toenails, you'll be able to see the quick as a pink crescent.

━━━━━━ TIP ━━━━━━

Skunk Odor

If your dog has had a skunk encounter, bathe her with shampoo, then soak her thoroughly with tomato juice. Massage the juice into her coat and leave it for a few minutes before rinsing completely. Repeat if necessary. If you don't have tomato juice, you can use strong lukewarm coffee. Instant coffee is convenient for this use.

apply a styptic pencil to the end of the nail (this will sting a bit), or dip the nail in a bit of flour. Gentle pressure with a small piece of tissue or cotton for about five minutes will also stop the bleeding.

Anal Sacs

The anal sacs, which are located on either side of the rectum, produce an odiferous substance that is expressed with a bowel movement. If the sacs don't empty, the dog becomes uncomfortable and often scoots on the ground or chews at its rectal area. If your English Setter seems to have this problem, have your veterinarian check her anal sacs and express them if necessary.

TRAINING YOUR ENGLISH SETTER

A well-trained dog is a pleasant companion; a poorly trained—or untrained—one makes even dog lovers cringe. Take the time to teach your English Setter basic obedience commands. You'll both have fun and the teamwork that training requires will strengthen the bonds between you and your canine pal.

Training Tools

Don't try to train your dog without the proper equipment. You'll need a training (choke) collar, the chain kind with a ring on each end. To determine the correct size, measure around the widest part of your dog's head and add 1 inch (2.5 cm). The lead should be made of webbing or leather, one-half to one inch (13–25 mm) wide and 6 feet (1.8 m) long.

Many owners argue that choke collars are cruel and dangerous. Properly used, a choke collar is neither. Constant tension is never used; rather, the trainer quickly applies just the amount of correction needed at the precise moment it is needed. When the correction is finished, which is a matter of seconds, the collar loosens to its original position.

Your English Setter will be a happier, better-mannered companion with a little training.

The choke collar is formed into a loop by pulling the chain through one of the rings. The lead is attached to the other end. Since the dog will be working on your left side, the loose ring—the one with the lead attached—of the collar should be on the right side of the dog's neck, having come across the back of the neck, not under the neck, and through the holding ring. This lets the collar loosen immediately when the pressure from the lead is released.

Rules of Discipline

Every dog will need some discipline and correction during training sessions. The amount of correction required depends on your dog's personality and whether or not you've previously allowed your setter to get away with misbehaving. If this is the case, your corrections may have to be quite strong, especially at first, to demonstrate that you're serious about your request.

Your primary discipline tools will be your voice and the training collar. Reprimands (a simple *"No!"*) should be spoken firmly without shouting. Corrections with the collar and lead consist of a short snap, a quick jerk on the lead, followed by *immediate* release. It's better to repeat the snap than to maintain the tension on the lead.

TIP

Specialty Training

Training an English Setter for hunting and hunting events is a difficult and lengthy process. Although some owners are capable of training their dog for these activities, most will achieve better results if the training is done by or with the supervision of a professional trainer. Your local English Setter Club, kennel club, or veterinarian may be able to refer you to a competent trainer.

Do not strike your English Setter, unless he threatens to bite you. In this case the correction must be immediate and forceful enough to let your dog know this behavior will not be tolerated under any circumstances. Threatening to strike your setter isn't acceptable either, even if you don't actually intend to hit him, because it will make him hand-shy. And never discipline your dog after he has come to you. He won't understand why he's being disciplined; he'll think it's because he came to you.

It's important to praise your English Setter as soon after a correction as possible. Find something that he's done right, then praise him and pat him. This lets him know his earlier misbehavior caused no permanent rift in your relationship.

Basic Obedience Training

Wait until your setter is about six months old before you start training. It's hard for younger puppies to focus their attention for the length of time required for training sessions. If your dog is older, even much older, than six months old, go right ahead with the lessons—you *can* teach an old dog new tricks.

✔ Training sessions should take place in an area where you and your English Setter have room to work. At first, your training spot should be free of major distractions, such as barking dogs and shouting children. Later on, your dog needs to learn to ignore these distractions and pay attention only to you. Limit your training periods to one or two per day. Start with five-minute sessions and gradually work up to fifteen to thirty minutes. After each lesson, take a few minutes to play with your student.

✔ Schedule your sessions for times when your English Setter is likely to cooperate. For instance, he probably won't be able to concentrate very well if the lesson takes place immediately after you arrive home from work. If your setter seems too bouncy for a training session, try taking him for a brisk walk or run beforehand.

✔ During the training session, position your English Setter at your left side. The lead should be held in your left hand, with any excess loosely coiled in your right hand. Give your commands in a clear, firm voice, always preceding the command with your dog's name (*"Basil, sit!"*). With commands such as *"Heel,"* when the dog will move with you, step with your left leg first. With commands such as *"Stay,"* where your dog will remain stationary, step with the right leg first. This will give your setter important cues about what he's expected to do.

Correction: Correction consists of a snap, with only as much force as needed. Remember to praise your setter when he does what you ask and also after every correction. Let him know that you expect your command to be obeyed immediately and that correction will always occur if it isn't.

Heel

To teach the *heel,* position your English Setter at your left side and start walking, left leg first, as you give the command, *"Basil, heel!"* Lightly snap the lead to encourage him to walk beside you with his neck and shoulder about level with your left leg. Continue encouraging him with light snaps, praising after every snap. If he charges ahead, give the lead a quick, light snap and repeat the *heel* command. Repeat the snap and command as often as needed, but never put continuous pressure on the lead. Practice heeling in short, brief sessions. Once your English Setter has mastered straight-line heeling, work on turns, circles, and maneuvering around obstacles.

Sit

Some trainers teach sitting and heeling at the same time. For the *sit,* the dog sits at the trainer's left side, facing straight ahead with head and shoulders square to the trainer's knee. When heeling, the dog sits whenever you stop moving, unless you give another command.

While your dog is heeling, stop walking and simultaneously give the command, *"Basil,*

To teach the sit, push your setter's rear quarters into a sitting position while holding the head up with the lead.

sit!" Let go of the lead with your left hand and use this hand to guide your dog's hindquarters into a sitting position. At the same time, hold his head up with the lead in your right hand. Praise him when he sits. Have him remain sitting for a few seconds, then give the *heel* command and start walking, left foot first. After a little more heeling, stop again and repeat the sitting exercise. Gradually increase the time your dog stays in the sitting position. Eventually, your setter will sit whenever you stop walking.

After your English Setter has mastered sitting during the *heel,* you can teach him to sit from other positions. Use the same command and positioning action that you used during the *heel.*

Stay

During a *sitting stay,* the dog remains in a sitting position until released by the trainer's command. Have your English Setter sit by your side, then give the command *"Basil, stay!"* and step a few steps away from

Puppy or adult, sitting still or bounding through the field, the versatile, athletic English Setter is sure to capture your heart.

him, right foot first, while holding the lead. Repeat the command. If he tries to come with you, tell him *"No"* and put him back into position. Have him stay for about 10 seconds. Continue working until your setter will stay for at least three minutes with one command. When this has been mastered, gradually increase the distance you move away.

Stand-Stay

The *stand-stay* is a *stay* where the dog remains in a standing position. First, you'll teach your dog to stand from the *heel*. While heeling, stop and simultaneously give the command, *"Basil, stand!"* As you give the command, use the lead to stop your dog's forward movement. At the same time, keep him from sitting by blocking the forward and downward

movement of his rear quarters, putting your left hand just in front of his right rear leg. You don't need to grab the leg; just block its movement. If Basil tries to sit down, start walking again and try the *stand* command after a few steps. Once he stands instead of sits, repeat the *stand* command and then give the command to stay. Continue this until your setter will stand at your side when you give the command. After a while, combine this work with normal *sits* during the *heel*. You want your English Setter to learn that the *sit* is required when you stop moving, unless you give another command. This is pretty complicated for the average dog, so you'll need to spend some extra time on this lesson. When your setter gets confused, be generous with your reassurance and praise any sign of compliance.

Now it's time to move away while your English Setter *stands* and *stays*. With Basil in a standing position, give the command to stay and move away, right foot first. If he tries to follow, tell him *"No"* and put him back in position, repeating the *stand* and *stay* commands. Continue until you can move to the end of the lead. Don't stay too long (a few seconds), then return to praise your student and release him from the *stay*. Repeat the lessons until he will *stand* and *stay* for at least one minute.

More advanced work on the *sitting stay* and the *stand-stay* consists of walking away and circling your setter while he stays in either the standing or sitting position. Hold the lead while you circle, making sure that it doesn't

With a little maneuvering on your part, your English Setter will soon understand what the command "down" means.

tighten or drag across your dog's face or other sensitive areas. It's all right if your dog turns his head to watch you, but he shouldn't change body position. If he does, correct him, repeat the command, and leave again.

Down

To teach this command to your English Setter, have him sit by your side. Kneel down and reach over his back with your left arm and grasp his left front leg near the body. At the same time, grasp his right front leg near the body with your right hand. Give the command *"Basil, down!"* and position him by lifting his front quarters off the ground and easing his body down. This maneuver is designed to prevent any struggles. He won't mind having your arms around him and he won't be able to resist the command by bracing his front legs. Once your setter lies down, slowly let go of his legs and let your left hand rest on his back, repeating the *down* command. After a few seconds, release him, and have him sit to try it again. Continue working until you no longer have to do any maneuvering. Then work until your English Setter will lie down while you remain standing. Finally, repeat the *stay* lessons while your dog is lying down.

Come (Recall)

To teach your setter this important command, put him in a *sitting stay* and move to the end of the lead. Kneel down and, in your most enthusiastic voice, say *"Basil, come!"* Hold out your arms, pat your knees, do whatever you can to coax him to you. He will probably come bounding up to you. When he reaches you, quickly give the command to sit, guiding him into position if necessary. Have your setter sit for a few seconds, then praise him. Continue working like this, gradually increasing the distance you move away before recalling him and using a longer lead, if necessary.

Some trainers teach the dog to assume the *heel* position on command as part of the *recall*. While your English Setter sits in front of you after the *recall*, give the command to *heel*, and use the lead to guide your pupil in a clockwise circle around you until he is at your left side. Then give the command to sit. For distractable dogs, the circle can be made out to your left, so you can watch your dog throughout the maneuver. Keep working until your setter will automatically assume the *heel* position when you give the command after the *recall*.

Working Off Lead

Once your English Setter has mastered the basic obedience lessons on the lead, it's time to work off lead. Before you unsnap that lead, however, be sure your dog will obey all of your commands without hesitation. To work off lead, have your setter sit by your side, then take the lead off and conduct a regular training session. If your dog makes mistakes, put the lead back on and correct as necessary. Concentrate your training on the areas where the problems occurred, then remove the lead for another try.

BREEDING YOUR ENGLISH SETTER

Your English Setter is everything you ever wanted in a dog. Sally's beautiful, intelligent, athletic—the list of outstanding traits goes on and on. One day you decide Sally should have a litter of puppies. What a great idea! Or is it?

Why Do You Want to Breed Your English Setter?

It's only natural to want puppies that are just like their mom, but unfortunately, there's no guarantee that Sally's puppies will be just like her. And if they are, will they truly be outstanding English Setters? Is Sally an outstanding English Setter or is she "just perfect" only in your eyes? Ideally, only the best examples of any breed should be allowed to reproduce.

Raising puppies is a big responsibility. You'll have to select a quality mate for your female (bitch), make sure she has adequate care during gestation and whelping, care for the puppies if their mother cannot, and eventually find suitable homes for them.

Each day, thousands of dogs and puppies are killed because there are no homes for them. Responsible dog owners don't breed their dogs

Puppies are cute, but they're a lot of work, too.

simply because puppies are cute or they want their children to experience "the miracle of birth."

If, after considering all these factors, you feel that your English Setter is special enough to pass on her genetic traits *and* you understand and accept the responsibilities involved in breeding her, you may decide to go ahead. Or you may decide to have your English Setter spayed. The decision is yours.

Choosing a Mate for Your English Setter

Even if you don't think your English Setter puppies will ever be shown, you should try to produce the highest-quality puppies possible because this will improve the breed. Generally, the best mate will be a dog that is a proven show dog or field dog and sire. The stud's record as a sire will tell you about his puppies and the type of bitch he crosses well with. An experienced English Setter breeder can help you judge a dog's quality and suitability as a mate for your setter.

Before you start looking for a sire, make a list of characteristics that you'd like the puppies to have. (There's no guarantee the puppies will inherit these characteristics, but the likelihood of it is usually increased if one or both parents possesses them.) Then check with your local kennel club, ask your veterinarian, or consult dog magazines, which contain advertisements for dogs at stud, to find dogs with these desired characteristics. Once you've identified several desirable dogs, evaluate their pedigrees, show records, sire records, and the dogs themselves. It's easiest to evaluate the dogs in person, but photographs and videotapes can also be used.

The stud dog's owner will usually want to learn more about your English Setter. After all, the stud's reputation depends on his puppies, so the owner must pick the mates carefully. You should have your bitch's pedigree and photographs available to show the stud owner. If your setter has a show or field record, you should have that available as well.

You'll need to find out about the terms and cost of breeding. Breeding to a top-quality proven dog can be expensive, but breeding to a younger dog is often more reasonable. Sometimes the stud dog owner is paid with one of the puppies ("pick of the litter") instead of money. In this case, the stud owner selects the puppy, usually the best of the litter. If only one puppy is born, or survives, it belongs to the stud owner.

Care of the Bitch Before Breeding

The stud owner may require veterinary certification that your bitch is sound for breeding and free from sexually transmitted diseases like brucellosis, which can cause infertility and abortion. Even if the stud owner doesn't require it, your English Setter's health and general condition should be evaluated by your veterinarian. She should be checked for internal parasites and treated, if necessary, and receive any immunizations that are due. Your veterinarian can also draw a blood sample to check the mother-to-be for brucellosis.

Bitches have their first estrus ("heat") sometime after the age of about six months. The bitch is fertile during this time. She will accept the male only during estrus. The estrous cycle recurs every seven months or so. Menopause does not occur in female dogs, but fertility declines in later years.

Male dogs become capable of fathering puppies sometime after the age of six months, reaching mature fertility shortly after one year of age. Males remain fertile for eight to ten years or more; they are able to breed females at any time during this period.

You shouldn't breed your English Setter during her first estrus. Pregnancy and lactation are detrimental to a bitch that is still growing. It's best to wait until your setter is fully mature.

The Mating Game

Females are usually bred about 10 to 14 days after the start of proestrus, the stage of the estrous cycle characterized by a bloody vaginal discharge. If your English Setter accepts the male, she's in estrus, the peak time for mating and conception.

After mating, it's normal for the male and female to be "tied" to one another for about 10 to 30 minutes. The tie occurs when the bulbous glands of the penis are temporarily entrapped in the vagina. Don't try to separate the dogs—you could hurt them. The male usually maneuvers around until he steps over the female's back to face the opposite direction.

The bitch will allow other dogs to breed her throughout the entire estrus phase, so it's important to keep all male dogs except the chosen stud away from her during this time. Don't make assumptions about any male dog's capabilities, as they're all potential fathers, regardless of age or size.

The Waiting Game

Now you've got about nine weeks to plan for the big day. As soon as possible, talk to your veterinarian about gestation and whelping. This will give you the opportunity to ask questions before a problem occurs. As the due date nears, you'll probably want to review the basic whelping procedures.

You don't need to change your English Setter's diet as long as you feed nutritionally balanced dog food, but you will need to increase her ration as her weight increases (see the chapter on feeding, beginning on page 41). Nutritional supplements usually aren't necessary. As always, keep plenty of fresh water available at all times.

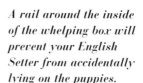

A rail around the inside of the whelping box will prevent your English Setter from accidentally lying on the puppies.

Decide early where the puppies will be born. If you don't, your setter might choose your white-carpeted living room or your bed as a site for her nest! Build or buy a whelping box early so your bitch has time to get used to it. The box should be large enough to let her stretch out full-length. The sides should be low enough that she can easily step over, yet high enough that the puppies cannot escape. A rail or shelf on the inside walls will prevent the dam from accidentally trapping a puppy against the wall. Line the box with newspapers or washable towels or rugs.

Whelping

Gestation length is really only an average, so you're not going to know exactly when the Big Event will occur. Even if you knew the exact time of fertilization, your English Setter could whelp 59 days later and still be completely normal. Tak-

ing the mother-to-be's temperature rectally twice a day, starting one week before her expected due date, will give you an idea of her timetable. A *one- to two-degree decrease* in rectal temperature means that whelping will occur in the next 24 hours.

Parturition: As parturition nears, the bitch will become restless and intensify her nesting activities. She will often refuse food, vomit, shiver, and/or whine.

Make sure you have everything ready:
✔ The whelping box, which your English Setter has already been using as a bed, should be lined with clean newspapers and/or towels.
✔ Prepare a smaller box lined with a heating pad and towel for the puppies, if needed.
✔ You'll also need sharp scissors and suture material or dental floss for tying off umbilical cords, if necessary; extra towels for drying the puppies; and your veterinarian's phone number and the number of a back-up veterinarian in case you cannot reach yours.
✔ Now that you're ready, remind yourself that your assistance probably won't be needed. As much as possible, let your setter do it herself.

After each birth: After each puppy is born the mother will usually tear away the amniotic sac and clean the puppy. If she doesn't remove the sac, gently pull it from around the puppy's face. The mother will also chew through the umbilical cord. Don't interfere unless she tries to bite the cord too close to the body, which may injure the puppy. If the mother doesn't break the umbilical cord, tightly tie some suture material or dental floss around it about 1 to 2 inches (2.5–5 cm) away from the body and, using disinfected scissors, carefully cut the cord on the side of the knot *away* from the body. The end of the cord that's attached to the body can be swabbed with a tincture of iodine to prevent infection.

An afterbirth (placenta) is usually delivered with or after each puppy, although two placentas may be delivered after two puppies. The dam will usually try to eat the placentas. Eating more than one or two may give her diarrhea or lessen her appetite for her usual diet. Count the placentas to make sure all of them have been deliv-

To you, your English Setter is the best. If you want to breed her, however, she should be a truly outstanding example of the breed.

ered. A retained placenta can cause a serious uterine infection.

If possible, leave the puppies with their mother even if she hasn't finished whelping. Puppies often nurse within minutes of delivery, stimulating release of oxytocin, a hormone that strengthens uterine contractions. Watch to make sure the new mother doesn't accidentally lie down on a puppy (she probably won't).

Don't get impatient if your setter wants to rest a bit, sometimes for hours, between puppies. If she seems comfortable and is caring for her puppies, she's doing fine, even if she's got more puppies to come. How long the whelping process will take depends on the number of puppies, the environment, and individual variation. The entire event usually takes less than about six hours, but there have been reports of uncomplicated deliveries that lasted 24!

When to Call the Veterinarian

Whelping problems are relatively rare, but there are some signs that indicate trouble. Call your veterinarian if your English Setter has not delivered a puppy after:

1. Two hours of intermittent contractions (first puppy).

2. One to 1½ hours of marginal nonproductive straining after the delivery of a puppy or the appearance of a water bag.

3. Thirty minutes of sustained contractions.

You should also call your veterinarian if your setter has an odiferous vaginal discharge or a

Instead of show-ring credentials, a Llewellin English Setter may have a field-trial record.

dark green vaginal discharge before she delivers any puppies—in between puppies, a greenish discharge is normal—or if she doesn't deliver a placenta for each puppy.

Caring for the New Family

When the delivery is completed, replace soiled bedding in the whelping box with clean dry towels, rugs, or a blanket. Check to make sure the box is in a warm, draft-free spot. Place some food and fresh water outside the whelping box, then go away. Mom can take over from here.

You'll probably want to take the new family to the veterinarian the day after whelping. Your veterinarian will examine the new mother for signs of retained placentas or puppies, bleeding, or uterine infection. The puppies will be examined for birth defects, whelping injuries, and general overall health.

Your setter will handle most of the puppy care over the next three weeks. You'll need to keep the bedding clean and free from puppy-trapping folds. You'll also need to make sure that each puppy is nursing and growing. Report any abnormalities to your veterinarian. Check your English Setter's mammary glands for heat or hard swellings, which could indicate an infection called *mastitis*. Also check for any abnormal, foul-smelling vaginal discharge. If you detect any of these signs, consult your veterinarian.

Eclampsia: Some bitches develop a serious complication called *puerperal tetany (eclampsia)*, caused by low serum calcium levels. The disorder is more common in smaller breeds, but can occur

in any breed. It typically occurs within the first few weeks after delivery when lactation is at its peak, but it can also occur prior to delivery. It is relatively uncommon in bitches fed adequate amounts of a nutritionally balanced dog food. Signs of *puerperal tetany* include restlessness, whining, staggering, increased heart and respiratory rates, increased body temperature, and, if untreated, convulsions and death. If your English Setter develops any of these signs, get her to a veterinarian immediately. She will need intravenous medication to correct the electrolyte imbalances caused by *puerperal tetany*.

Dewclaw removal: Dewclaw removal is usually performed by a veterinarian when the puppies are less than a week old. This procedure, while not an AKC requirement for English Setters, eliminates the painful problem of snagged and torn dewclaws.

Raising Orphan Puppies

If the mother cannot or will not take care of her puppies, you'll have to do it. The job only lasts for two to three weeks, but it can be time-consuming, especially with large litters.

Warmth

The puppies will need a warm, dry bed, such as a small towel-lined box. Place the box in a draft-free area. Place a heating pad underneath the bedding or hang a heat lamp above the box. Adjust the heat source to provide warmth without overheating. Position it so some areas are warmer than others. The puppies can choose where they're most comfortable. Ambient temperature should be 85 to 90°F (29–32°C) for the first week, 80 to 85°F (26.7–29°C) for the second through the fourth weeks, and 70 to 75°F (21–23.9°C) for the fifth and subsequent weeks. Relative humidity should be about 50 percent. Pans of water placed near the heat source outside the box will help maintain humidity.

Since orphaned puppies sometimes suck on one another, some experts recommend providing a separate box for each puppy. If you isolate each puppy, you'll need to provide sufficient heat for each box. If you keep the puppies together, watch closely for sucking, and separate the puppies if it occurs.

Feeding

You'll need to feed each puppy nutritionally balanced milk replacer, available from your veterinarian or pet supply store, for a few weeks.

You can feed the puppies with a small animal nursing bottle, an eyedropper, or a syringe. Feeding instructions for the replacer can be found on the label or you can consult your veterinarian. In general, if the replacer has an energy value similar to that of bitch's milk, you'll need to feed a total of about 13 to 17 mL per 100 g of body weight per day for the first two weeks. For the

third and fourth weeks, if the puppies aren't self-feeding by then, increase the ration to about 20 to 22 mL per 100 g bodyweight per day. Divide the total daily amount into four or five equal feedings. For the first few feedings, reduce the amount a bit to allow the puppies to become accustomed to the replacer.

Technique for feeding puppies: When it's time for a feeding, get everything ready first. You'll need freshly made up milk replacer—a day's supply can be made up and stored in the refrigerator—warmed to about 100°F (37.8°C). You'll also need cotton balls and warm water. Place the appropriate amount of replacer in the bottle, syringe, or eyedropper, then pick up the puppy and wake it up, if necessary, by massaging it and talking to it. If you're using a bottle, hold it so the puppy doesn't swallow air. If you're using a syringe or dropper, hold the puppy upright in your hand, then place the end of the syringe or dropper in the puppy's mouth and slowly dribble in a little formula, then wait until the puppy swallows it. It'll take a while for the puppies to learn to eat this way. Continue feeding until you've fed all the formula or until the puppy stops eating, which is usually a sign that it's full.

Elimination: For about two weeks after birth, newborn puppies urinate and defecate in response to the dam's licking, so after every feeding, wipe each puppy on its anal/genital region with a cotton ball moistened with warm water. When the puppy urinates and defecates, wipe it away with the cotton ball.

Weight: Weigh the puppies every day for the first week so you can tell if they're gaining weight. This will also let you know if you need to increase the amount of replacer; the puppies will need more as they grow. The puppies' weights may decrease in the first two or three days, usually due to the restricted feedings, but they'll soon start gaining. After the first week, you'll need to weigh the puppies only once or twice a week.

Observing the Pups

At first it may be difficult to tell how the puppies are doing, because newborn puppies don't really do too much. However, even a newborn puppy should wiggle when you pick it up. After learning to eat, each puppy should readily consume its meals. A puppy that's not snuggling with its littermates may be weak or sick. A sick puppy may have labored breathing, coughing, nasal discharge, and diarrhea. The stools will be soft while the puppy is eating milk replacer, but they shouldn't be watery. Have your veterinarian check any puppy showing any of these signs. Regular weighing will also help you evaluate each puppy. A puppy that's not gaining as fast as the others may be sick, or it may just need more to eat.

Moving the Pups

When the puppies have their eyes open and are more active (about two weeks), you can move them to a bigger box. The box should have sides that are high enough to keep the puppies from climbing out. Continue to provide a heat source for them. You can also start offering them replacer in a large shallow dish before every feeding. They'll mostly walk in it at first, but they'll soon figure out what it's there for. Once the puppies learn to lap from the dish, they can take all of their meals that way.

Weaning

When the puppies are four weeks old, you can start weaning them. Make a gruel of dry puppy

food soaked in puppy milk replacer. Put it in a large unbreakable saucer, then put some of it on your fingers and wipe it on the puppies' mouths. Use your gruel-soaked fingers to lead the puppies to the saucer.

As the puppies learn to self-feed, gradually increase the thickness of the gruel. When they're easily eating thicker gruel, start using more water and less replacer until you're mixing the dry food with mostly water. Your goal is to have the puppies eating dry puppy food, but that will probably take a few weeks.

Preventive Care

Your puppies should have their first immunizations at about six weeks. Your veterinarian will also want to check a stool sample for internal parasites. Keep a record of immunizations and other veterinary care, so you can give it to the puppies' new owners.

Adoption Time

Soon those babies will be eight weeks old and you'll need to find homes for them. But *don't* send any of them off unless you are certain that the new owner will provide the absolute best of care—for a lifetime. Interview each prospective owner to make sure he or she understands the responsibilities of dog ownership, including the necessity of providing food, shelter, grooming, veterinary care, training, and companionship. The prospective owner should have a responsible attitude toward dog breeding and population control. If you have any doubts, don't give up the puppy at any price. The last responsibility you have to your puppies is to find each of them the best possible home.

HAVING FUN WITH YOUR ENGLISH SETTER

It's not hard to have fun with your English Setter. In fact, there are so many different kinds of fun the two of you can have together, you might have trouble deciding what to do first.

Tricky Business

Once your English Setter has mastered the basic obedience commands, you and your pet can start developing a repertoire of tricks. Shaking hands and rolling over are classics, but dogs can also be taught to play dead, hold the end of their own leash, or even another dog's leash, balance objects on the end of their nose, and many others. "Speaking" and "singing" are popular, but a dog that doesn't know when to finish the conversation or sing the last chorus can be a real nuisance!

Most bookstores and public libraries carry books about training dogs to do tricks. If you know someone who has taught his or her dog to perform tricks, you might ask for help with your training efforts.

Physical Fitness

Your English Setter will probably enjoy walking or jogging with you. Consider your dog's comfort as well as your own during these excursions. Don't overdo the exercise during hot weather,

Sometimes having fun means just being together.

especially if it's also humid. It won't hurt to walk or jog in the rain, but remember to dry your setter off when you get home. Walking or jogging in moderately cold weather shouldn't cause many problems—the exercise will help you and your setter stay warm. If you walk or jog on snow, check your dog's feet frequently for balled-up snow. Be sure to wash any snow-melting compounds off your setter's feet when you get home.

Fun and Games

Playing ball with a dog is an activity almost anyone can enjoy, regardless of age or physical limitations. Your English Setter won't mind if you don't throw very well, as long as there's a ball to chase. See the chapter on raising your setter for guidelines about selecting a safe ball (page 33).

Dogs also enjoy playing Frisbee. Some of them become quite adept at it, performing super-canine contortions and spectacular leaps in pursuit of the soaring disk. If you decide to play Frisbee with your setter, make sure you play in a grassy or sandy area that's obstacle-free, to decrease the chance of injury should either of you fall.

Dog Clubs

Dog clubs are found in many large towns and cities. In sparsely populated areas, dog clubs may include members from a wide region of the state. In addition to regular meetings, dog clubs often hold puppy matches, unrecognized (by the AKC) dog shows that help inexperienced dogs or owners prepare for the competition of recognized shows. For information about dog clubs in your area, contact AKC Customer Service, 5580 Centerview Dr., Raleigh, NC 27606 (919-233-9767). A local dog breeder, pet supply store, or veterinarian may also be able to help you find a club near you.

Canine Good Citizens

Any dog, even one that's not AKC-registered, or even purebred for that matter, can earn a Canine Good Citizen Award. This AKC-sponsored program was developed to encourage dog owners to teach their dogs basic good manners. Dog clubs throughout the United States administer the Good Citizen test, which includes situations such as allowing a stranger to approach, walking naturally on a loose leash, sitting for an examination, and other tasks. The dog that successfully completes the pass/fail test receives a Canine Good Citizen Certificate. For more information about this award, contact the AKC for

TIP

Organized Activities

Your community may offer some organized activities that you and your English Setter may enjoy. These activities may range from simply belonging to the local dog club to more complicated and time-consuming ventures, such as showing in recognized dog shows or obedience trials.

the name of a dog club in your area that sponsors this evaluation.

Dog Shows

An AKC-registered English Setter that's not neutered or spayed can be shown in AKC-recognized dog shows, obedience trials, and other activities, such as field trials and hunting tests. Altered dogs can't participate in dog shows, but are eligible for all of the other events.

In a dog show, each dog is judged according to its official AKC Breed Standard. Dogs initially compete against others of the same breed, gender, and age. Class winners continue competing until one dog is selected as Best of Breed, the dog that most closely exemplifies the Breed Standard. The judge then selects the Best of Opposite Sex. These dogs—the top male and female of their breed in the show—are the only dogs of their breed that receive points. After a dog wins Best of Breed, it then competes against the other Best of Breed winners in its AKC Group (Sporting Group for English Setters). The winners from each group competition then compete against each other for the title of Best of Show, the highest honor awarded in a dog show. When a dog wins a certain number of points at AKC-recognized shows, it earns the title of Champion (Ch.), which is added to the beginning of its name.

Trials

Obedience Trials

In AKC obedience trials, performance is the only thing that counts. Obedience classes are organized into Novice (easiest), Open, and Utility (most advanced) categories.

The English Setter's gentle personality and love of people make it a good candidate for certain types of service work.

✔ In the Novice class, the dog performs basic exercises, including heeling, standing for examination, long sit, long down, and recall.
✔ In the Open class, the dog performs more advanced exercises, such as heeling free, retrieving on the flat and over a vertical obstacle, and broad jump.
✔ Utility classes require the most advanced obedience tasks, such as responding to hand signals, scent discrimination, and directed retrieval exercises.

To earn an obedience title, a dog must earn three "legs," which are awarded when the dog scores a certain number of points on each exercise and overall in the competition. Obedience titles include Companion Dog (CD) at the novice level, Companion Dog Excellent (CDX) at the open level, and Utility Dog (UD) at the utility level. Only dogs that have earned the Utility Dog title can become Obedience Trial Champions.

Field Trials and Hunting Tests

If you'd like to show off your English Setter's hunting ability, check out AKC-sponsored field trials and hunting tests. Field trials are competitions in which certain members of the AKC Sporting Group or Hound Group demonstrate their hunting ability. The trials are conducted separately for the pointing breeds (like English Setters), retrievers, and spaniels in the Sporting Group. Pointing breed field trials are conducted on a single course with or without a bird field—an open area where game birds or pigeons are released—or on multiple courses with or without bird fields. Several levels of progressively more

advanced competition are offered, including puppy stakes, derby stakes, gundog and limited gundog stakes, and all-age and limited all-age stakes. Dogs are judged on qualities such as hunting style, game-finding ability, obedience, pointing, steadiness on point, and honoring. The titles awarded for achievement in field trials are Field Champion and Amateur Field Champion.

Hunting tests are open to all AKC-registered English Setters and other pointing breeds, retrievers, and spaniels. Hunting tests are not competitions, but evaluations of the dog's ability in several categories related to hunting performance. Only qualifying or nonqualifying scores are given. The hunting test is conducted on a single course with or without a bird field or solely on a bird field. In the junior hunting test, dogs are scored in categories of hunting, bird-finding ability, pointing, and trainability. Dogs in the senior hunting test are evaluated in the same categories (greater proficiency is expected), as well as the additional categories of retrieving and honoring. In the master hunting test, dogs are evaluated in categories of the senior test, but are required to demonstrate additional refinements. Successful completion of the respective

Hiking can be lots of fun with an English Setter, a dog that thoroughly enjoys the great outdoors.

hunting tests earns the dog the titles Junior Hunter, Senior Hunter, and Master Hunter.

Service Activities

Dogs are increasingly being used to enhance the health-related activities of hospitals, care centers, and rehabilitation centers as researchers discover the health benefits of the human–dog relationship. Most of the time, these dogs are owned by people who volunteer their time and the companionship of their special canine friend.

Service dogs must be well-mannered and reliable. They should respond to people calmly without jumping up, barking, or biting. Service dogs shouldn't be frightened by unusual sights, sounds, smells, or activities. They must, of course, be completely housebroken.

English Setters are well suited for certain types of volunteer work. Most are affectionate and responsive. As a breed, English Setters are energetic, but with a little training many of them can be quite calm when they're on duty. The setter's bounciness may actually be an asset in some situations, such as engaging a patient in activity. Few people can resist an English Setter's invitation to play.

In some cities, organizations have been formed to train and coordinate the activities of volunteers and their dogs. Some of these, such as Support Dogs of St. Louis, Inc. of St. Louis, Missouri, offer training courses that the dog and owner must attend before they can be assigned to a facility. The dog is taught to tolerate the activities, smells, and sounds that it may encounter during its work. When the dog/owner team has successfully completed the training course, it is assigned to regularly visit a hospital or other care facility.

To find out more about volunteer opportunities for you and your English Setter, contact hospitals and care centers in your area. If they don't have this type of program, they may know of a facility that does. Or they may be interested in starting a program. Talk to volunteer agencies. Also, your veterinarian may have information about volunteer programs. Keep trying until you find the opportunity that's just right for you and your setter. Service activities are a truly special way to touch the lives of others with an English Setter's love.

INFORMATION

International Kennel Clubs and Registries

American Kennel Club
51 Madison Avenue
New York, NY 10038
212-696-8200
www.akc.org

For registration information:
American Kennel Club
5580 Centerview Drive
Raleigh, NC 27606
919-233-9767

The Field Dog Stud Book
The American Field Publishing Co.
542 S. Dearborn Street
Chicago, IL 60605

United Kennel Club
100 E. Kilgore Road
Kalamazoo, MI 49001-5598
www.ukcdogs.com

National Breed Clubs

English Setter Association of America, Inc.
Dawn Ronyak, Secretary
114 S. Burlington Oval Drive
Chardon, OH 44024
www.esaa.com
(This address may change with the election of
new officers. Contact the AKC for the most
current address.)

Organizations

American Society for the Prevention of Cruelty
to Animals (ASPCA)
441 E. 92nd Street
New York, NY 10128
www.aspca.org

American Veterinary Medical Association
930 N. Meacham Road
Chicago, IL 60173
www.avma.org

Books

American Kennel Club. *The Complete Dog Book.*
New York: Howell Book House, 1992.
Baer, Ted. *Communicating With Your Dog.*
Hauppauge, NY: Barron's Educational Series,
Inc., 1989.
Campbell, William E. *Owner's Guide to Better
Behavior in Dogs and Cats.* Loveland, CO:
Alpine Publications, Inc., 1989.
Faculty and staff of the University of Califor-
nia-Davis School of Veterinary Medicine. *The
University of California-Davis Book of Dogs:
The Complete Medical Reference Guide for
Dogs and Puppies.* Siegal, Mordecai and Jef-
frey E. Barlough, (eds.). New York: Harper
Collins Publishers, 1995.

Periodicals

Dog Fancy
P.O. Box 53264
Boulder, CO 80322
303-786-7306

Dog World
29 N. Wacker Drive
Chicago, IL 60606
312-726-2802

INDEX

Photo Credits

Kent and Donna Dannen: pages 2–3, 4, 9, 12, 16, 17, 20, 24, 25 (right), 28, 32, 33, 36, 37, 40, 44 (top), 45 (right), 48, 52, 56, 57, 60, 65, 68, 76 (top), 77 (top right, bottom left, bottom right), 80, 84, 85, 88, 92; Tara Darling: pages 8, 25 (left and bottom), 44 (bottom), 45 (left), 72, 76 (bottom), 77 (top left).

Cover Photos

Front cover, inside front cover, inside back cover: Kent and Donna Dannen; Back cover: Pets by Paulette.

About the Author

Karla S. Rugh earned her D.V.M. from Kansas State University in 1974. She also holds a Ph.D. in physiology and has advanced training in veterinary anesthesiology. She has practiced veterinary medicine in both private and academic settings. Dr. Rugh is currently a freelance writer and writing consultant. Having enjoyed the companionship of many dogs, she admits that choosing her favorite breed would be a difficult task.

Important Note

This pet owner's guide tells the reader how to buy and care for an English Setter. The author and the publisher consider it important to point out that the advice given in the book is meant primarily for normally developed puppies from a good breeder—that is, dogs of excellent physical health and good character.

Anyone who adopts a fully grown dog should be aware that the animal has already formed its basic impressions of human beings. The new owner should watch the animal carefully, including its behavior toward humans, and should meet the previous owner. If the dog comes from a shelter, it may be possible to get some information on the dog's background and peculiarities there. There are dogs that as a result of bad experiences with humans behave in an unnatural manner or may even bite. Only people that have experience with dogs should take in such an animal.

Caution is further advised in the association of children with dogs, in meetings with other dogs, and in exercising the dog without a leash.

Even well-behaved and carefully supervised dogs sometimes do damage to someone else's property or cause accidents. It is, therefore, in the owner's interest to be adequately insured against such eventualities, and we strongly urge all dog owners to purchase a liability policy that covers their dog.

© Copyright 2000 by Barron's Educational Series, Inc. Illustrations © Copyright 2000 by Tracy Flickinger.

All inquiries should be addressed to:
Barron's Educational Series, Inc.
250 Wireless Boulevard
Hauppauge, NY 11788
http://www.barronseduc.com

International Standard Book No. 0-7641-1495-6

Library of Congress Catalog Card No. 00-039815

Library of Congress Cataloging-in-Publication Data
Rugh, Karla S.
   English setters : everything about purchase, care, nutrition, and behavior / Karla S. Rugh.
      p. cm. — (A complete pet owner's manual)
      Includes bibliographical references (p.).
      ISBN 0-7641-1495-6 (alk. paper)
      I. Title. II. Series.
   SF429.E5 R84   2000
   636.752'6–dc21   00-039815

Printed in Hong Kong

9 8 7 6 5 4 3 2